True Confessions

of a

Clairvoyant

True Confessions

of a

Clairvoyant

by

Angela George

Michaelangelo

Publications

A MICHAELANGELO PUBLICATIONS BOOK

True Confessions of a Clairvoyant
by Angela George

Published by
Michaelangelo Publications Ltd
Box 20-110, Christchurch, New Zealand

angiepangi@xtra.co.nz

First published and printed 2007
Copyright © 2007 Angela George
First English Edition

The moral rights have been asserted

Editor:	Caroline Martin
Design:	Graphics, Cover and Layout
	Michael Cole – *Michaelangelo Design Studios Ltd*
Printed:	Zenith Print
Bound:	Zenith Print - www.publishme.co.nz
	www.sellmybook.co.nz

Self-help / Spiritual category
ISBN 978-0-473-12936-1
A catalogue record for this book is available from the National Library of New Zealand

Ecological policy:
Michaelangelo Publications makes a concerted effort to ensure that the materials and processes used to produce each edition follow sustainable guidelines.

Dedication.

To Mum and Dad - with love.

♥♥♥♥♥♥♥

Contents

Acknowledgements

I wish to express my appreciation to:

Michael Cole, for his encouragement and love throughout this writing process. I thank you for assisting me when I struggled to clarify the various principles and for sharing your excellent design skills. I am forever grateful for the growth and love you so readily give me.

Erica and Charlie for choosing me as their mother this lifetime. I admire you both for standing by your own truths and for the depth of your values and integrity.

Bruce Martin, my friend and mentor, who many years ago gave me a Parker pen for Christmas. I so admire your compassion, patience and depth of love for mankind.

Heidi Collins, who after reading my first draft, demanded I allow her to promote and market this book so that everyone throughout the world could access these principles. I have always loved your enthusiasm and strength of belief.

Robyn Bottomley, who kindly assisted me with my grammar. Thank you so much.

Caroline Martin for her editing and proof-reading skills. You have a fantastic way with words, a lot of tact and a wonderful sense of humour.

Anne de Lautour *for recognising the importance of publishing this book. Thank you for going that extra mile for me.*

Pauline Taylor *thank so much for your encouragement and incredible expertise that you gave so unconditionally.*

All the staff *at Publishme.com who are friendly, helpful and warm every time I phone.*

Finally I would like to thank all my clients for choosing to spend time with me, thus offering lessons and growth for my soul.

Foreword

I was delighted when Angela asked me to write the foreword to her first book, **True Confessions of a Clairvoyant**. It gives me an opportunity to share with you some of the remakable insights that I have gained during the time that we have spent together.

I became aware of Angela's presence many years before we actually met. I used to see her amazing blue eyes peering at me whenever I used to meditate deeply. But strangely enough, I didn't recognise her when we met face to face. At the time I was Director of the College of Natural Medicine in Christchurch and Angela arrived at the College with a mutual friend to organise some evening talks. Needless to say, the courses were very successful and many of the students and staff subsequently went to her for clairvoyant readings. I always marvelled at her amazing ability to see beyond the physical world and we talked for hours about spiritual stuff. She even dragged me along to listen to her hero, Stuart Wilde, when he visited New Zealand and insisted that I read his amusing books about energy and personal transformation. She thought that, because I was English, I was too serious and that I should express myself more! Gradually we became good friends, I learnt to laugh more and we enjoyed mentoring each others' inner growth.

Angela was invited to Thailand by a woman called Alice and I was asked to come along as well. So began one of our many adventures. We boarded a plane and flew to Chang Mai not knowing if our friend would be there to meet us. At Bangkok we found ourselves without some important papers we needed in order to pass armed guards on the gate that led from the International part of the airport. We decided the solution was to become invisible! So the Kiwi blonde, English gentleman and our laden baggage trolley walked straight past the two officious-looking guards. We really had become invisible to them - it was absolutely astounding! They both did not see us although we were in full view!

During the trip we experienced many of these miracles, past life flashbacks, synchronicities, epiphanies and a wonderful feeling of intense spiritual growth. I was constantly amazed by Angela's ability to consistently read anyone. I remember that she did some readings for a group of Thai bankers and through an interpreter told them secrets that only they knew! I then realised that the mysterious world of spirit is totally connected across all cultures, beliefs and languages. How does she do it? She has reminded me many times that it does not involve the thinking mind but intuition. This requires inwardly asking, listening and feeling. She assures me that the ability is there within each one of us.

Although I had read a number of books that had been channelled, I had never directly experienced it until meeting Angela. She would lie down as if going to sleep and I would sit, pen in hand, waiting for her to speak. But the voice that came from her relaxed body was not the everyday Angela that I knew so well. The words that she now spoke were poetical, full of unconditional love and incredible wisdom that seemed far beyond her waking personality state. I tried taping the conversations that I had with this 'other' Angela, but on playback, it was only my voice that could be heard asking the questions between the audible hiss of blank tape. I thus became known as 'the scribbler,' who wrote pages and pages of wisdom that poured out during these hour-long sessions. The waking Angela became known as the 'host.' The voice did not have a name, but Angela called the presence the 'Old Codger.' At the end of each session Angela would awaken, but strangely could not remember what she had said.

The 'Old Codger' is a part of Angela's higher being and is the source of her accurate and powerful readings that you will read about in this book. Each of her sessions was usually recorded on a tape deck. However, some of her clients would call her back to say that her voice did not come out on their tape. There were many excited clients who phoned years later saying that everything she had said on the tape had actually happened for them. Remarkable!

Over time, Angela wanted to expand beyond the one-on-one approach that had been the format of most of her readings. So we developed an inner awareness programme that we originally taught in Asia and New Zealand. It was called *Connecting with your Higher Self*. The workshops were not only extremely popular with our students, but they also enabled us to continually grow and evolve ourselves. Many of the techniques that we employed have come about as a result of the channeling and insights gained from her readings. Angela has threaded much of this wisdom into the stories within this wonderful book.

True Confessions of a Clairvoyant will take you into the mysterious and intriguing world that I have described. Angela provides you with an insider's view, not only of the processes that happen during a session, or while listening to the messages from those who have passed on into spirit, or forecasting future events. In reading this book you may rediscover a purposeful direction within your life. Her stories, humour, anecdotes and bursts of wisdom are legendary.

The search for hope and clarity is why many of us make the trip to the clairvoyant's door. Those who found her door, also found love, laughter and wisdom. Most people want the *spook reader* to become the channel for messages that they have not yet learnt to either hear nor see. "When will I find my soulmate? What does my future hold? Will this job suit me? How can I get out of this crisis? My mother died recently. Is she OK?", and so on…. The answers, it seems, lie not only all around us, but are also awaiting discovery within each of us.

Within the pages of this book Angela shares many of the remarkable stories that she experienced during her professional career. We see each of her clients through her clairvoyant vision as they struggle with the challenges they faced. Angela's insights from every story are remembered and explored with the same mixture of compassion, humour and directness that brought clarity and direction to each of her clients. In sharing each story she shows us a deeper view of the underlying lessons and the Universal wisdom that pervades each of her sessions. In seeing the stories through her eyes, we are privileged to catch a glimpse not only of how these lessons and insights assisted her clients at the time, but also of how we can now apply the techniques and answers within our own lives.

We are, according to Angela's guidance, the real masters of our own destiny, magicians of universal energy, who are continually creating our own future. But she reminds us that we are also the masters of our own downfall. Negative thoughts lead to poor choices and even worse results. However, assistance is always at hand, and Angela provides us with a simple guide to purposeful self-determination in the form of Universal Laws. In doing so, she squarely, lovingly and humorously places the responsibility for our individual destiny in our own capable hands.

Michael Cole

Introduction

I have wanted to write this book, **True Confessions of a Clairvoyant**, since the early '90s but to be honest with you and more importantly myself, (this is the first of many confessions I will make) I have simply procrastinated. As I look back over this period, I can't help but notice how much I have changed and therefore grown; so I guess, in hindsight, the time is right for me to put pen to paper or rather fingers to a keyboard. As I myself have changed and evolved, so too has the aim or purpose of this book, and by the time it is published, I will have grown even more because of the experiences this process in turn has given me.

In taking you with me on my journey, I hope to promote a greater awareness of universal love and share my experiences within the spiritual realms, so that you might choose to expand the wonderful potential and possibilities you already have inside. I strongly believe in the importance of taking responsibility for all aspects of your life. In doing this, you will automatically connect to the master within, thus becoming the creator of your own destiny. In the end, it all comes down to self-love, love for others and for all living things. Through my life experiences I came to understand that this love was not to be found outside me, it came from within, and once I understood this I realised I would never be alone.

I believe we live in two worlds, the physical world and the spiritual world. Aspects of the spiritual world are constantly present in the physical world and send many messages. These are available to us all and come as gifts, but we must be aware enough to recognise them. Synchronicities and coincidences have meaning, and there is always a connected thread that runs through our lives. In fact, our life is but a tapestry and we are linked into the lives of others, even if we are not aware of the threads.

I have chosen to write this book in three sections. The first part is about my childhood, and includes significant milestones on my journey to enlightenment. I am, of course, still constantly evolving like everything else in the world. My purpose in sharing this is so that you will see some of the similarities between us. We are all products of our own families and are influenced by different family members throughout our lifetime. Maybe by reading my journey you will experience some revelations about yourself.

In the middle section I relate the stories of some of my many memorable clients; for privacy reasons, I have changed their names. In the final section, I share Universal Laws I have benefited from, and which have given me a greater understanding of life. Sometimes they are the reverse of how people see the world and I refer to these in the first two sections. At the end of the book is a reference section called Spook Terminology, where I explain the meaning of the various terms I have used.

I have been asked countless times how old was I when I realised I was clairvoyant. My second confession is that I was unaware I was any different from anyone else until halfway through 1988. Yet now, as I look back over my life, I would have to agree I was aware of certain psychic phenomena, but at the time, I thought, so was everyone else.

So join me at the beginning of my life's journey and enjoy the similarities or revelations we may share together along the way.

1
My Journey to Now

♥ *My early childhood*

♥ *My journey into enlightenment*

My Journey to Now

My early childhood

I was born a Capricorn, in the year of the snake, according to Chinese astrology. The younger of two girls, growing up in suburban Christchurch, New Zealand, I believed I was a typical Kiwi kid. My father was born in South Africa, my grandparents having emigrated from England approximately three years before his birth. When Dad was 19, his father was posted to New Zealand by the British company he worked for, and he and his family moved into a house three doors down from my mother's family, on Cashmere Hills, overlooking Christchurch.

Mum was the oldest of four children, all born in New Zealand, though her grandparents on both sides were immigrants from Ireland. Mum and Dad met each other at the bus stop halfway between the two homes. Other than his parents, the only family Dad had ever known was his sister, whereas Mum and her siblings had parents, countless aunts, uncles and cousins. Mum had been brought up a Catholic, whereas Dad had no religious affiliations.

Within two years of his arrival, Dad had enlisted in the New Zealand Army and served five years and 19 days, mainly in

Egypt and Italy. In 1947 they married at the local Anglican Church, and Mum gave up her Catholic faith forever. My sister was born three years later and I arrived three years after that, with a supposed heart defect. To this day I'm not too sure what the defect was, but suffice it to say I received a clean bill of health by the time I started school. I do recall my parents and other family members being concerned about my health, yet somehow, deep inside, I always knew I would be okay.

As Mum was the only one of the four children who married and so had children, my sister and I were especially treasured by her extended family. Because of Dad's career, my parents were often out of town, sometimes out of the country, for up to three months at a time, and, from as early as I can remember, my sister and I spent countless days at our second home with Mum's family.

During my time as a preschooler the majority of people around me, including my family, were always commenting that they couldn't understand what I was saying; and so at an early age I learnt not to say much but just to observe. I didn't bother asking questions when I wanted to know something because more often than not, I wasn't understood. Instead, I learnt how to feel what was going on by connecting with the atmosphere and energy around me. I knew instinctively when things were on an even keel and when they weren't. I got to know when adults were saying one thing but feeling something different. I watched as their children behaved in a similar vein and I understood why they did. At this early age I learnt to believe in what I felt and not in what I heard.

On my first trip to the school dentist it was discovered I was severely tongue-tied. In fact it wasn't just my tongue, it was my whole mouth. After surgery, I attended a speech clinic for a year and, as I excelled in this area, Mum encouraged me to take up elocution lessons, hoping it would help overcome the shyness I exhibited. My love for poetry and plays, which grew out of the elocution lessons, lead me into drama classes, and I would spend hours learning poetry or the lines of a play I was involved in. Looking back over my childhood, I believe I had to suffer the experience of being tongue-tied, to learn the art of entering this other world which surrounds us all.

On Banks Peninsula, 80 kilometres east of Christchurch, is a holiday resort village called Akaroa. In 1956, my parents bought a little over half an acre of land just above the beach, in the middle of the township. These days Akaroa is a thriving tourist and affluent holiday destination, but back in the '50s, when land was cheap, couples would buy plots and knock up rough and ready kiwi baches or cribs. So, like many Kiwi kids, we watched Dad, sometimes through trial and error, build our family bach.

My sister and I would wait patiently until he finished the job of the day, then he would take us to the beach for a swim. Always on the way home we would walk along the path by the local school, where Dad said the fairies lived. Each time he told us a different story about what the fairies were doing. I recall wishing that I could see them as clearly as Dad could. Sometimes, if I closed my eyes and then opened them again really fast, I could convince myself I saw them amongst the trees and bushes, just as Dad described them. Often I'd swear I heard them call my name, just like he said they were doing. I believed him when he said there would come a day when I would see them clearly.

Dad didn't have to read books to us because he was such a clever storyteller; he had an amazing fund of stories in his head and somehow you never heard the same story twice. Knowing about the fairies in Akaroa was possibly my first introduction to believing in the magical world, a world we all can visit, if we are aware that it exists. Sometimes I would pretend I could see fairies at the bottom of our Akaroa garden. I believed they were my friends and I would spend hours in this world of fairyland making wishes and telling them everything I felt inside.

Looking back, I realise that opening myself up to this world of fairies also allowed me to see the world of pain that human behaviour creates. As a child I often felt frightened by what I felt, never knowing how to cope with what these feelings meant. Often I would cry for no apparent reason and of course my communication skills were somewhat limited because of being so severely tongue-tied.

When I was about five or six, one of my great aunts moved into a prominent old people's home, run by the Catholic Church, which had an orphanage on the top floor of the building. Every Sunday when we were at our second home, our grandparents would take us to visit her. I dreaded going there and each time we pulled into the driveway I would go through the ritual I had created within my mind, in the hope of convincing myself that this time it would be different, but it never was. All I wanted was to be able to behave like my sister, who appeared to be so unaffected by the atmosphere we were walking into.

Often we would see some of the orphans; I could never look at them, but instead felt their pain and sadness. Sometimes I would cry for no reason, and at other times I shook uncontrollably as I tried desperately to hide behind my big sister. I would hang onto her out of sheer fear, knowing I was in for a telling-off from my grandmother for behaving so badly in front of the nuns, but I could never give a reason for why I did it. All I knew was that I was so frightened of being hurt by some adult.

Now, as time has revealed, I realise that I was picking up on the pain and sorrow that existed within that building. Years later, the old building was pulled down, which to me was a blessing, for it shifted the energy that lingered there. Interestingly enough, it was after the building was pulled down revelations of the physical and sexual abuse that had occurred there became public knowledge. Buildings always hold the truth of the energy of events and circumstances that occur within. Often it is the children who are able to pick up the feelings in the atmosphere, even if they are oblivious to their meaning. This is when children learn to lie, to put on a brave face, because of the need to conform or fit in with others in order to be liked and accepted. Sadly, this is learnt by the time they become adults.

Years later, I had a female client, who had spent her childhood in the orphanage during the years I had visited my great aunt. Her early childhood experiences confirmed to me what I had known as a child visiting there, but which I had been too scared to voice.

I had another great aunt on my mum's side, Auntie Maggie, who was 80 when I was born, though she didn't seem nearly that old. She taught me how to knit clothes for my dolls and we chatted endlessly over the knitting and jigsaw puzzles we did together. I loved her dearly, as she did me. Often in our chats I would tell her how much I would miss her when she died and how much I feared her leaving me. I remember I was in the sunroom knitting a burgundy skirt for my walkie-talkie doll, when she promised she would come back to see me after she died. We made it our secret and it was never mentioned again, because I knew she would, for she had promised me.

In the November, before my seventh birthday, I asked Mum if we could visit Auntie Maggie as I hadn't seen her for some time. After many excuses she finally told me we couldn't go because Auntie Maggie wasn't well. No amount of pleading would change Mum's mind because, according to the adults, Auntie Maggie was not well enough to see children. Weeks later my parents didn't have to tell me she had died, for Auntie Maggie had kept her promise to me. The day after she died, I woke to see her by the side of my bed. With her thoughts she advised me all was well and I was not to fear, for she would never leave me, even in death.

I didn't tell anyone until Dad came home from work in the middle of the day to pick Mum up to go to Auntie Maggie's funeral. I knew they didn't believe me; they thought I must have overhead them talking. Unbeknownst to me, I had perfected the art of picking up the spirit of those who had passed over. I spoke to her often after she died. The adults around me didn't understand this and so I learnt very quickly to converse with her by thought, or when I was talking to the fairies at Akaroa. (It is while I have been recalling these past memories that I have realised the day Auntie Maggie died is the same day, 21 years later, on which I last saw Dad alive.) The tapestries of our lives never cease to amaze me! But let's get back to my childhood.

After a couple of years of elocution lessons, I became more

confident at public speaking and loved reciting the various poems I had learnt off by heart. I enjoyed the plays we performed as a group and lost my shyness around people. I guess by the time I was 10 I considered myself too old to converse with the fairies. From then on I looked forward to my teenage years and all the fun there was to be had with real friends. I changed schools and by the time I was 12 my social life was taking off. I learnt how to ice-skate, listened to the Beatles and the Rolling Stones and, like all other teenagers, sang the hit songs of the '60s and '70s.

Because my parents were in their mid-30s when they had me, they were conscious of being older than many of my friends' parents. They were both very sociable people and enjoyed the company of my friends. If I didn't ask my friends home, they would, and so for the Christmas holidays our house at Akaroa was always full of teenagers. The days were spent out in Dad's boat, fishing and water-skiing and at night Dad would light the barbecue and Mum would make the salads.

Through these years the other world I had lived in during my early childhood lay dormant. Outwardly, it appeared Dad was the most influential parent of the two, but it was really Mum who subtly influenced many of my subconscious behaviour patterns in these formative years. Dad was the more outgoing one and had no difficulties at all in expressing his love, whereas Mum was less forthcoming, as was the case with her family members, but you could still feel the love from them all.

One of the many lessons Dad taught me was the importance of joy and laughter in my life. As I said earlier, Dad was a great storyteller and all his stories were laced with humour and often highly embellished; anything to make the listeners laugh longer and, in the case of children, to stretch their imagination just that little bit further. To Dad, life was to be enjoyed and to be filled with as much joy and laughter as possible. No matter what the situation was, he could always find the positive, rather than focusing on the negative.

To illustrate this I shall share a story with you. In the early days there were no fences around our property in Akaroa, mainly because of the cost and the fact that our land and surroundings had originally been part of a farm. In our back yard we always had livestock belonging to the farmer next door; therefore, the grass was kept under control without a lawnmower. As the years went by one of the neighbouring properties changed ownership and the new neighbours wanted to erect a fence between their property and ours. They offered to put the fence up if we paid half the timber costs. Dad agreed gratefully, as it was one less job for him to do. Dad was fairly well-known and liked by the locals, and so when the neighbour boasted about having put the fence further into our property, thus giving him more lawn area, it wasn't long before Dad was made aware of the situation.

The area in question was well away from our bach, so instead of confronting the chap about pinching some of his grass, Dad saw it as someone mowing part of his lawns for him and often referred to the neighbour as his gardener. When questioned by others as to why he had allowed this, Dad's argument was that he was not robbed of his land, as it was still his by law, but that this neighbour was maintaining it for him and, what's more, his maintenance work was for free. Dad had the last laugh when the neighbour attempted to sell the property, but that's another story.

This was one of the many lessons I learnt from my dad that

too often we get caught up in negative thoughts of what so and so did to me, spending our time on things that really are of no consequence when we could so easily spend it on far more important matters like having fun.

Dad loved to play tricks on the people around him; anything for a laugh, he'd say. The problem was, sometimes he pushed others just that little bit too far. He spent hours in magic shops whenever he was in Australia, always coming back with tricks to play on some poor, unsuspecting individual. He always had in mind a particular person when he purchased a trick. Each prank involved an element of risk and was planned down to the minutest detail; and he had the knack of keeping a straight face and looking totally innocent as he played it out. He loved it when someone played a joke on him and he often used to take someone else's prank and adjust it for his own use. While Dad played the joker, Mum sat back and cringed at his actions.

Dad applied these skills in his career and was well-known as a pioneer within the business world. If someone told him his ideas would not work, he'd make it his mission to prove them wrong. One of Dad's favourite sayings was 'extraordinary people do extraordinary things and I will always be extraordinary. I don't like crowds'. He loved the adrenaline rush, I believe.

In hindsight, it was the night Dad died suddenly of a stroke, that I revisited my childhood world. I was pregnant with my first child, due to give birth within the month, unable to sleep; yet I felt calm and peaceful knowing that, while I had only spent 27 years with Dad, I knew my time with him was not over. Another of Dad's favourite sayings had been 'Once you're dead, you're dead, so make the most of your life, whatever you do'. But I knew that night his understanding of life and death had changed. I knew, because I felt him so strongly in my bedroom with me, very much alive but not of his physical body.

After my daughter was born, I felt him around me every moment of every day. Yes, there were times of great sadness and grief but through it all I knew he would never leave me. I spoke to him constantly, sometimes jokingly, sometimes out of anger and frustration at him for dying, yet I knew he would remain around me. That I was certain of. I might add, I would never have got away with half the abuse I flung at him if he hadn't been in that other realm! Often he would answer my question with a knocking or creaking sound somewhere in the room and, at night, the lights would flicker. I lived in this reality as days turned into weeks, then months. Somewhere inside, I knew to keep Dad's visits to myself.

About six months later, Raewyn, a friend of mine, suggested I accompany her to an evening with a medium from England. I was so excited and thought of nothing else, demanding that Dad make his presence known and come through with a message for me; Dad didn't let me down. The medium picked Dad up in spirit form and confirmed his daily presence with me. With the messages I received that night, I knew I had embarked on a journey, although I had no idea how, or when, I would reach the destination. In fact, I didn't even know if there would be a destination. Nor did I care, because I knew Dad would be with me.

Twelve months later my son was born. I spent the first year of his life sharing with my sister, the responsibility of nursing Mum, who had terminal cancer. The three of us made an unspoken pact to keep Mum at home rather than let her go to a hospice. Yes, there were times when one or all of us would feel stretched, but somehow we found the strength to carry on. Even now, as I look back on those months and the treasured times we shared, I wouldn't have done it any differently. There was not a day that passed when I didn't feel Dad's presence, especially when Mum's health was very low. The lights would flicker, the jug would mysteriously start to boil and the house would creak. I had no doubt it was Dad, though Mum and my sister were not so convinced.

One of the most memorable moments happened one night about nine o'clock, after I had fed, bathed and put my children to bed and settled Mum for the night. Having only had about five hours' sleep over the previous two days, I was exhausted, yet surprisingly calm. As I sat in the living room, I looked up at the photo of Dad on the wall, asking him to please make sure they all slept that night so that I could catch up on my own sleep. To this day, I swear Dad's image changed as he flashed me a broader smile than the image his photo portrayed. I jumped up and went to pour myself a whisky, in the kitchen, when suddenly the lights flickered and the jug started to boil. I poured the whisky down the sink and headed up to bed, knowing Dad would grant my request.

The next morning Mum told me in explicit detail of the dream she'd experienced of being with Dad. I shared my encounter of the night before with her, and from that moment on Mum constantly asked me if I truly believed she would see him again. I admitted, for the first time, the promise Auntie Maggie had made to me and explained how I knew when she had died. I guess it would be fair to say that given Mum's condition, it was understandable she would want to hold onto this belief, but for whatever reason, we made a similar pact with each other.

Mum passed away peacefully in the next two months and I waited patiently for her visit. Those who have spent time with a cancer patient, will know the aroma that lingers around them. I sometimes smelt this in the bedroom Mum had slept in when she had visited me in my own home; I would open all the windows thinking the aroma was still in there. However, I didn't feel her presence as I had with Dad, nor did I become aware of any obvious signs.

About six months after Mum died I applied for a position with New Zealand Television, a position Mum and I had often spoken about. The producer of the programme agreed to give me an opportunity, and, as the doors of the lift in the building shut, I smiled to myself as I asked Mum out loud what she thought. The familiar aroma which filled that lift confirmed to me that she knew and was proud of the fact that I had achieved my dream. I knew then she was with Dad.

Through the many experiences I've had with the spiritual realms, I've realised that the traits people exhibit during this life are still with them when they reach the other side, including all vices and virtues. Sadly the death of the physical body offers no guarantee of enlightenment. I believe all souls are given the opportunity to learn more about love, but traits don't necessarily disappear on entering the spiritual realms. Whenever I picked up the departed during readings they would show me particular traits they'd exhibited as earthly beings, thus confirming their presence to the clients. For example, I had two sisters who came to see me. Their father showed me an image of himself tending cactus plants in a hothouse. On relaying this to them, I was told of the important position he had held in the Cactus Society.

But back to my story. Once I was drawn to visit my parents

at the crematorium. It was at a stage in my life when I was debating what direction I should take to move forward in my life. I was at sixes-and-sevens over this decision, knowing that by moving in the direction opening up for me I would be stepping out of the norm. I could count on the fingers of one hand the times I've visited the crematorium, purely because I don't believe they are there. I sincerely believe they are with me wherever I am, especially if I ask them to be with me.

Nevertheless, I found myself beside the rose bed, full of yellow peace roses which they shared with others. A gardener was in the process of digging up the rose that grew above their nameplate. He apologised profusely to me, explaining that this was the third peace rose he had planted, yet for some reason the rose always flowered with shades of pink spotted on the rose petals. I stood there laughing, knowing at last what my decision was to be – to step away from the norm!

I realised that, even in spirit, Dad couldn't bear to fit in with those around him. I don't know how many times their rose has been replaced since then, but I suspect the gardeners finally gave up changing it. Last time I visited them I couldn't help but smile at the pink-spotted yellow peace rose which stood so proudly above their nameplate amongst the other yellow ones.

The thing I missed the most when Dad died was his love – his love for me, for people, for animals and for everything life can be. He had an immense passion for life and for what you could learn from living. He was a great humanitarian and there was nothing he wouldn't do for someone, should they ask. As the years have gone by, I have begun to know that this love is with me always; and so is Dad, with Mum right beside him. It was Dad who introduced me to the other world when I was a child, and it was he who brought it back to me when he died.

My journey into enlightenment

Before having children I had a career in hospitality, travel and tourism; and when my son was three, I was offered part-time work in the industry. After the sharemarket crashed in October '87, the travel business diminished and I was not required during 1988. With more time on my hands, I began my search again in an attempt to understand the different scenarios I was experiencing. I found myself amongst a variety of new-age believers, palm readers, tarot readers and astrologists all searching for some understanding of spirituality. I had always been fascinated by palmistry and so decided to learn more about it. I borrowed books from the library on the subject and scoured various bookstores, hungry to learn all I could.

Back in the late 1980s, I thought past lives and reincarnation were concepts only found in Eastern countries. I had never been interested in Asian religions or belief systems, so my knowledge of these philosophies was very limited. I had no idea if there was any truth in these concepts; they were never in my reality, nor had they been mentioned to any great degree in my limited knowledge of religious teachings. I had been christened an Anglican and had attended an Anglican Church school from the age of 11. For the seven years I was there I sat through two compulsory periods a week of what was called Divinity, though I paid little attention, and thus had a very limited knowledge of my so-called religion. In fact, for most of my life I considered religion something of a waste of time and certainly had no space for it in my life.

My dear mother paid a donation to the local Anglican Church each year, but as a family we never went to church. An amusing story my father loved to tell was of a plane flight when he sat next to the long-standing vicar of this church, who told him that being an airline passenger was the closest he would ever get to heaven. The only time I ever saw my parents attend church was for a wedding or a funeral.

The concept of having perhaps lived another life, in another time, was not a belief I warmed to. In fact, whenever I heard anyone talking in this vein, I'd consider them to be in fantasy or la-la-land and I was more than willing to try anything to prove them wrong. One of my acquaintances had a friend who was a hypnotherapist. After a bit of persuasion I agreed to a series of weekly appointments with him.

After a while I experienced the feeling of being with my higher self, which I later realised was my soul. I found I could easily step back from my everyday personality to experience feelings of being in my soul's space; it reminded me of when I was a child. As the weeks went by, I dropped into this space consciously during my day-to-day life. I knew I had done this before because it felt very natural. On explaining this to the hypnotherapist, he told me I had the potential to further advance my intuitive side.

I recall the day he informed me there were not that many individuals able to achieve this state of being. I once again became very sceptical. I asked him how people knew where another person was at and what they were feeling or thinking if they couldn't attain this soul-space. It was at that point he called me over to the window, which overlooked a cobblestone area below. We were three storeys above ground level, looking down on a variety of people walking in various directions. He pointed to a woman wearing a red coat and carrying a black handbag. He asked me what was happening for her at that time. I put myself into my soul's space and realised she was heading towards the building on her left to pay her insurance, which was overdue, and this concerned her. As we watched her climb up the steps to the insurance office, a male came down the steps. When asked what he was doing, I said he was meeting his wife on the corner over to the right and that they were going to the bank to increase their overdraft.

I was somewhat surprised when the hypnotherapist informed me he would never have picked up any of those details and added that neither would most individuals. However, as we had no proof that any of my psychic guesswork was correct, I shrugged it off as pure imagination. Then he pointed to a woman and young child walking towards the building we were in and asked what I picked up from them. I informed him they had an appointment in this building, and within seconds I knew they were his next clients. He asked if I was aware of why they were coming to see him and I said that the son had a problem with bedwetting and was coming for treatment.

We waited until they arrived at the reception area and when the hynotherapist went out to welcome them, I overheard the conversation between them confirming this as the reason for the appointment. I reflected on this. As a child I had often known what other people's intentions were, although how I knew this I was never able to explain. I had truly believed that everyone was able to do what I did. This revelation about myself gave me a huge step forward in understanding my natural abilities.

Through my time with the hypnotherapist I uncovered a variety of past lives, but the one that stood out above them all was of me as a young Polish girl. I first saw myself as a starving waif in a concentration camp in Germany. When the hypnotherapist asked my name, I recited a number, claiming I didn't have a name any more, just a number. The feeling of fear and helplessness was overpowering; it felt like every ounce of hope had been squeezed out of me. I explained how we were all stamped with a number on our arm, and how we were all dressed in camp uniforms. I was terrified of the guards and the patrolling dogs. I was terrified of being alive and felt death would be a welcome escape. I lived with death and witnessed it all around me every moment of every day. I described the camp in great detail; later, as Angela, I discovered it was Dachau.

He then led me back to my earlier life before the camp. I saw my bedroom, describing the furniture and how it was placed in my room. I relived how my mother had died in childbirth along with my young sibling; I was an only child brought up by a loving Jewish father. There was a housekeeper, who also showered me with much love, and my bedroom was filled with dolls of all sizes, along with dolls' houses and clothes. My father was a journalist and everyday I would watch him from my bedroom window, walking down the street in his dark grey/black overcoat, carrying a small briefcase under his arm. He always stopped on the corner to wave goodbye. I knew this period of that lifetime was extremely happy for me, full of love, dreams and hopes for the future. Then the Nazis took my father from his workplace and three days later they came for me.

I relived the last day I saw him alive, the train ride to the camp, and the process of being admitted into the camp and being branded with a number on my arm. I recalled there was a man in front of me, possibly in his mid-30s, who would only put his right arm out to be numbered. I saw the guards hack his arm off and number him on the left arm as was regulatory procedure; he later died later because of the lack of medical treatment. Eventually, I died of starvation just before my 15th birthday, which was on 8 May 1945; a welcome release from the four years of hell I had lived through in Dachau.

When I came out of the regression I still felt intense hunger pains, so much so, I devoured the hypnotherapist's lunch. Knowing this life in Germany, I can understand why in this lifetime, as a young child, I was frightened of barking dogs – I didn't even have to see them to be scared, why I can't stand yesterday's bread; sleeping in bunk-rooms with lots of people; high fences on my property; lining up for food in restaurants with buffet-type menus; and why I always cook more food than is required. In fact, it is a family joke that when we go on holiday, I need to find the nearest supermarket to stock up on food. When I am hungry I need to eat and so my fridge and pantry are always full of food . . . yet another family joke. Many weeks later, after some research, the hypnotherapist told me that the number I had mentioned to him was the number of a young Polish girl whose first name was Esther.

But to bring us back to my own journey this lifetime. Once I was aware I was on a spiritual journey, I attracted to me similar like-minded individuals and, in no time at all, I found myself surrounded by new-age believers all searching for some understanding of spirituality. There were astrologists, numerologists, hypnotherapists, tarot-readers and palm-readers. Amongst them was a group of individuals, who, in their spare time, ran a programme on a local radio station, focusing on the paranormal. To raise money to pay for this programme, they had organised a psychic fair at the Christchurch Arts Centre and I was asked if I would do some palm-reading for them. I was adamant I could not read palms, but agreed to attend and assist in organising the day.

As soon as I arrived I was led into a booth, along with the first client, and told to go for it. As I sat down, I was told the client would pay $5.00 for 10 minutes; I just had to say what I saw. Too embarrassed to do anything else I complied with the request. I remember the first client's face even now, a male in his mid-60s; I looked into his eyes, blanked my mind and took his palm in mine as I called on my parents to help out. I spoke about his fly-fishing in the Waimakariri River; I described his two daughters and the grandson whom he took fishing at the Rakaia River, where his caravan was parked. Through me, his wife, who was in spirit, commented on the different colours of the geraniums she had once planted just outside the caravan door. Before I knew it, the bell went and his time was up. I let go of his palm, sat back in my seat and said "Now that was a bit of fun, wasn't it?" The look on his face told me that it had been more than just a bit of fun for him.

I read palms every 10 minutes for the next six hours and I must confess I enjoyed every one of them. I had so much fun dipping into the lives of all those people at 10-minutes a go. As I walked to my car to go home, a group of people surrounded me, asking for my phone number because they had missed out on a reading, and those that I had done wanted a longer reading with me. I shook my head in disbelief proclaiming that I didn't do readings – I was just having some fun. Suddenly, a young girl grabbed my arm and said I had given her a reading in the hall and that she needed to speak to me about the family crisis she was going through. I kept apologising and expressed how sorry I was, explaining that I was only having fun. To me, the whole thing was a laugh; I was in no position to advise her on any family issues.

About a week later, one of the organisers, who ran the radio station, rang to tell me they had had many calls from the public wanting my phone number. At that stage I was the family breadwinner, trying desperately to get back into the travel industry. As I wasn't having much luck on the job front, it was suggested to me that perhaps it would be a good idea if I looked at doing readings for some money. That suggestion, I confess, was the beginning of my practice as a palm-reader. The going rate at that time for fortune-telling was $30.00; it was better than no money coming in at all. I decided to give my clients a two-hour session for $30.00.

I would begin my readings by explaining to the clients how they had one of four types of hands – air, fire, earth or water. A person with a 'water' hand is usually sensitive, intuitive and creative; an 'earth' hand belongs to someone who is practical and down to earth; a 'fire' hand indicates someone who is an extrovert, active and excitable; whereas a person with an 'air' hand is intellectual, a great communicator and rather inquisitive. I would then describe what the shape and length of the fingers and thumb expressed about them. How the fingers 'sat on the hand' told me more about the person's character. The fingerprints and mounts on the palm revealed different psychological aspects within, indicating talents and abilities the client was born with and the strengths and weaknesses of character they had.

Then I would discuss the major lines, any important minor lines and finally I would trace the client's life, following the lifeline starting at birth. Every major event would be marked on this line – childhood, relationships, marriage and financial problems. For example, someone who'd suffered an abusive childhood, either mentally or emotionally would have islands and hair-lines running through the beginning of the lifeline. A dot on this line would always indicate a major life-changing event; for example, the beginning of sexual abuse, or the death of someone close.

By the time I had read the hand, the client and I would feel well acquainted. I loved every minute of it as I learnt and grew with every palm I read. So much so that I could hardly wait until I had the client sitting in front of me. I was so fascinated by what I could see in their lives. Another confession – the pictures I saw and the story I relayed to them had nothing to do with the lines on their palms. I could see many other aspects, just by having them sit in front of me.

After a few weeks, I realised I was losing out on would-be clients because they wanted the tarot cards read, not just their palm. So to rectify that, I confess, I bought a pack of tarot cards, learnt the meanings of the cards from the small booklet included in the pack, and three days later I combined palm and tarot readings together. Another confession – I could never remember the meanings of the cards. Instead, I adapted the spreads to suit what felt good for me. I laid the cards out and said what I saw in front of me. There were times when the client asked me which card expressed what I had just said. I would point randomly to one of the cards in front of me because I was too embarrassed to say that I didn't need cards to see into their future. Clients would sometimes ask me for the names of the books that had taught me the meanings and I would say, I couldn't remember, again too embarrassed to tell the truth. Oh, how I have changed. Now I would be more honest and admit what was happening for me.

While I ran a successful practice, growing spiritually with each reading, my personal life offered growth for my soul as well. Within seven years of Dad dying, my sister and I experienced the loss of our mother, two grandmothers, one of Mum's brothers and her sister. In between these six deaths, two close family friends passed away unexpectedly as well. My sister lived in Auckland and was married with two sons, while I lived in Christchurch and was also married with two children of my own. As the years went by, my sister's parents-in-law moved into a one-bedroom unit on the ground floor of her family home and she became very much a part of her husband's family. Unlike her, I experienced rejection from my husband's family and consequently there was little communication between us.

Eventually, I removed myself from this situation as I found the strength within to stand on my own. The sympathy and support I received from the friends around me made me even more determined to become self-reliant. I found within me the power of self-responsibility. I refused to be the victim of circumstances or of my situation, and I was determined to pass this new-found strength and courage onto my children. Yes, there were times when I felt fear, but I never gave up on believing in myself because I knew somewhere deep inside I could not afford to, for my own sake. I made a promise to myself to overcome these challenges and in doing so I could share this with others. I spoke to my parents constantly, sometimes pleading with them to help me by showing me signposts for the direction I should go in. The more I connected to them, the stronger I felt their presence.

In 1990, I started running workshops on self-worth and self - love, but it was during 1992 that I decided to stop my reading and concentrate solely on the workshops. Through them I taught the importance of self-freedom, how to connect with the master within and how to rely on the self for direction.

Yet I felt myself in conflict. It seemed to me that the majority of clients were looking to me for their direction, instead of themselves. I felt I was not really helping them if I gave them directions, because everyone knows deep inside what is right for them. Hence I decided not to take any more new appointments, but gave readings for the ones I had already made, which took me through to 5 August that year. I had no concrete idea of what else I was going to do, yet somewhere inside I knew my path would reveal itself. I was right, though I didn't see it too clearly at the time.

On the following day, a colleague rang wanting me to meet Alice, a French woman, who was visiting Christchurch. Alice lived in Phuket, Thailand; her husband, Seri, was Thai/Chinese. They had one son who attended St Andrews College. Alice was looking for a clairvoyant, and whilst I was adamant I would not do a reading, I nevertheless agreed to meet her. My meeting with Alice, three days later, heralded the beginning of a friendship that was to prove very deep, complicated and, may I add, intriguing. Alice had lived in Thailand for over 20 years; along with Seri, she had embraced the culture and lifestyle and become a fully integrated part of the Thai community.

Alice was a great believer in spiritual teachings and recognised me instantly, whereas I was oblivious to our connection. I guess it was because I was too busy trying to avoid doing a reading for her. Alice rang me constantly during her stay, always wanting to spend time with me, whereas I wanted to run in the opposite direction. What's more, I knew that she was well aware that I felt this way. Alice, being as direct as she is, confronted me, finishing the conversation with how she had recognised me from a past life and that I couldn't be that fantastic a clairvoyant if I hadn't realised the connection myself. She believed we had things to work through and complete within our soul-relationship. Often we would have similar dreams, and while spiritually we had a lot in common, we were also complete opposites.

I recall Alice having our astrology charts done, which showed proof of our deep connection at a soul level. There were times we frightened each other, times we argued and yet through these times the bond between us revealed its strength. Because of this we both knew we could never walk away from each other. Meeting Alice proved to be a huge turning point in my life. Through Alice I was invited to run a series of workshops in Singapore during 1994 and I grew incredibly through this experience.

I returned to Christchurch for good after three years of flying back and forth to Asia. I began my clairvoyant practice again with past clients, which in time led to new clients. Instead of running large groups over a weekend, as we had in Asia, my partner, Michael and I decided to put together a 10-week course, 'Conversations with your Higher Self.' Through our experiences in Asia, we had concluded that for universal laws to be fully integrated into a participant's life, our courses needed to run over a longer period.

So for the next six years we ran them in the evenings during the week, from our lounge, with 10 to 12 people in each course. In no time at all we were running courses four nights a week. We found that we grew along with the participants. By popular demand, we found ourselves creating two advanced courses, 'Creative Power of Love', followed by 'Voice of the Soul'. Michael and I coauthored workbooks, which contained information from our courses.

Even after the courses, we received enthusiastic reviews about the workbooks, and this feedback convinced me to once again change my career. Thus I purchased a laptop and began to write. I feel that in writing I reach more individuals, who have the same birthright as myself to know about this other world. I truly believe life should be lived to the fullest. When you know how to get the most out of life, I believe you will create circumstances for this to happen; thus you will feel fulfilled, for you will be living your soul's purpose. I once read somewhere a saying that went like this: 'Oh God, to have reached the point of death, only to realise you have never lived at all'. It is my belief that we are here to learn lessons. In learning them we come home to our innerselves, a state which is full of love and who we truly are.

So come along with me now as I share some amazing stories about some of the individuals I have met through my readings. Let us explore the gifts they have given me. You too can make use of these gifts as I have. If you wish to share them with friends, please, be my guest.

2
Don't Shoot the Messenger

♥ *For goodness sake, where is this all leading to?*

♥ *Blinded by judgement*

♥ *The day the Universe set me up*

♥ *Never too late to learn*

♥ *Our life is our own*

♥ *Putting your life on the line*

♥ *What! No answer?*

♥ *Clairvoyant mayhem*

♥ *God moves in mysterious ways*

♥ *Who's that in my ear?*

Don't Shoot the Messenger

It was during my experience as a clairvoyant that I realised I was purely a messenger, or a channel, for the spiritual realms to relay their messages to my clients. At first I found the readings a bit of a laugh, a fun-time to have with a client, but as time went on I realised the seriousness of being the reader. Males and females of all ages and walks of life came to see me and I valued the learning I received from each one. I loved the variety and I felt honoured that they allowed me into their personal lives.

One of the most frequently asked questions from friends and acquaintances has been "What kind of person would come to someone like you?" They would then add "People with lots of problems. I bet it must be so draining for you." Well, I can honestly say I have never ever felt drained after giving a reading. This is because, in every instance, I have connected to the universal energy, to hear or see what is to be passed on to the client. I have always felt very privileged to be chosen for this task and forever grateful for the experiences I have had with each client who has walked through my door. I have learnt so much about myself and have gradually understood more about the spiritual realms.

There have been times when I have said goodbye to a client, after a session and I have known they were thinking, "Well that was a bit far fetched." Some have even said, "Yeah, well it will be great if it happens!" Often in a reading, I have found myself asking "How could something like that possibly happen?" But I have learnt that what is to be said will be said; the spiritual realms know far more than I do. I do believe that there are many situations you can change in your future, but there are other situations that are meant to happen for the lessons and experience they will give you.

For goodness sake, where is this all leading to?

I soon discovered it was not the words I used that were beneficial; it was more the energy transference that made the difference. On principle, I refused to tell people what to do with their lives, which I know frustrated many a client, but I had no intention of running their lives for them as that was their responsibility, not mine. Whenever that was expected of me, which was often, I would simply ask my higher self to assist in bringing clarity to the client's reality. As a result of that I would find myself coming out with some seemingly absurd statements. At that point I would feel a surge of energy going through me and a realisation would occur within the client. That is what I mean by energy transference. It was not so much my verbal advice that was the trigger; I merely became a channel for some realisation or awareness from the spiritual realms. It was something unseen that was traded between me and the client and I always knew when such a realisation had occurred because we would both feel lighter. The client would see his or her life with more clarity and leave with new ideas or direction. It confirms how connected we all are.

Being clairvoyant comes with a price. For example, I often find the need to waffle about nothing to friends, family and often strangers. When I hear myself uttering this sort of mindless chatter, my personality will often kick in with 'Oh for goodness sake, where is this leading to?' Then the energy surges within me and the person I am having a seemingly mindless conversation with suddenly opens up about some aspect in their life they are searching for an answer to. I then shut up as the client talks, though I am well aware of the transference of energy that is occurring. Eventually, a 'eureka' moment occurs for the individual, right in front of me.

I often wonder why I find myself been drawn to speak to total strangers. I used to stop myself, but I now realise there is a reason for this behaviour and it is not for me to understand the reason, nor do I need a logical explanation. It is for me to follow and trust the directions that the Universe gives me. An example of this occurred recently. Over the past three months I have been drawn to chat away to one of the checkout operators at my local supermarket. Through our conversations she has told me she comes from a small town down south, left school at 16 and worked at a fruit and vegetable shop before coming to Christchurch to live. Each week I would hear the latest instalment about her teenage life – what she did in the weekend, what clothes she had bought, even the woes of her teenage friends – while she was swiping my groceries across the scanner and packing them into bags.

Three weeks ago I was standing with my trolley of groceries, looking for the shortest checkout line, when she called out to me to pick her queue. I lined up and waited for her latest update only to find that this time she was looking for some advice. Once she had trotted out the latest drama in her life she asked what I thought she should do. I heard myself waffling on about how important it was to be true to yourself and never compromise yourself. My personality kicked in with "She's not going to get this." Suddenly I felt this surge of energy as I heard her say that she was forever compromising herself with her friends because she wanted them to like her. By the time she had handed me the last bag of groceries, I knew by the look in her eyes that clarity had struck and she knew exactly what to do.

A week later I was back in the supermarket, when she came bounding up to me as excited as any 17-year-old can be, talking nineteen to the dozen about how she had sorted out three different scenarios that had bothered her for ages. One related to her friends, and her decision was to be honest with them about how she felt. Her reason for taking this action had stemmed from the words I had used – be true to yourself and do not compromise yourself for anyone. Brilliant, I thought, the Universe works again!

I believe in the idea that when individuals ask for help someone they know will pop into their heads. Next, they connect that person – it might happen either through a chance phone call, or an unexpected meeting – with the answer or information they require. There is a lot of truth in the saying 'Being in the right place, at the right time with the right company.' It is often the key to learning or acquiring what one needs for the next step forward.

Blinded by judgement
When I first started my readings, I used to be invited to different towns throughout New Zealand, where a local resident would organise sessions for me. I would arrive with my deck of tarot cards, be assigned a room in someone's house and away I would go. The readings would be booked two hours apart from 10am through to 6pm – four readings

a day over a period of eight to 10 days. As I had no family responsibilities at that stage, I was able to immerse myself completely in the inner realms. Whilst many assumed I would be exhausted, I was actually very high on universal energy. The more readings I did, the more in tune with the other realms I became. Often, the tape-recording of the reading would come out as a high-pitched sound whenever I was speaking, yet the client's voice was always as clear as a bell. This is why I often recommended the reader take notes, just in case.

One of my favourite stories is the time I was invited over to Greymouth, on the west coast of the South Island, where the readings were to be done at the home of a local fisherman and his wife. I began with the first client at 10am and had just begun the second reading at noon, when the door of the room burst open. The wife and two other women rushed in exclaiming that I had to leave immediately as the weather had turned and they had seen the husband returning in his fishing boat. The husband knew I was in town but not that I was doing readings in his sunroom!

I was bundled into a car with my cards and tape deck and taken to someone else's home, where I finished the 12 o'clock reading, and then driven to the local hotel, where I was assigned one of the bedrooms to do my readings. This room was on the ground floor, very close to the public bar. The two o'clock reading arrived at three, as I was behind schedule due to the change in venue, but no one seemed perturbed. By the time I emerged from the room at 7pm, I was very aware I was the talk of the public bar. I had caused quite a stir amongst the male locals.

Each day I would be driven back to the hotel to continue my

readings in the same bedroom. On the fifth evening I was invited to join the locals in the public bar for light refreshments, and I was subsequently coerced into extending my stay as various males, on hearing stories of my predictions from their wives, insisted on booking appointments with me.

The reading that is etched most clearly on my mind is the one I did for a fisherman. I thought he would be sceptical of my abilities and I assumed he would confront me with his disbelief; but it was quite the opposite. Ten minutes into the session, I knew by seeing the layout of his home in my mind's eye that it was his place I had been previously removed from. Shortly after this realisation, he bluntly told me he was not interested in the reading of the future. Rather, he was seeking confirmation that it was his mother's spirit he had seen as he came to after a recent operation. You could have knocked me down with a feather, as he willingly shared details of this experience. Within moments I felt his mother's presence, and as I relayed her messages to him, the tears began to flow. I was literally blown away by the emotions he shared with me. I realised then that I had judged him unfairly. I should have checked with my inner realms before proceeding with the reading. Oh what a valuable lesson this man had taught me!

The day the Universe set me up!
When I first started doing readings for people, I was very careful about what I told them. When I felt or saw something I believed to be negative, I would not refer to it but if asked, I tended to downplay the information. In fact, there were times when I would spend a lot of time and energy avoiding any negativity I was being shown. I had a fear of predicting disaster and I also had a tendency to feel responsible for the feelings of the client. Oh, how time and experience

changes one's outlook and perceptions! After a few months of readings, I was shown there was a reason for everything I felt or saw, and it was my responsibility to share this with the client; I had no right to censor what they should or should not hear. It was for me to trust and know that the Universe could see a much bigger and wider picture than I could.

After all my previous censoring, the Universe finally set me up for one of my greatest lessons. It was a Saturday afternoon and two women arrived on my doorstep together, wanting to sit in on each other's readings. I never minded this as I was aware some individuals felt more comfortable with a companion beside them, though I always asked them to tell me if I was picking up on the observer by mistake, as this could sometimes happen. These women were sisters and had lost both their parents in the Mt Erebus disaster, 12 years earlier. The father's sister had taken them into her family even though they were in their early 20s by then.

Both souls of the parents spoke to the sisters, and I heard their father expressing that they were not to worry about their aunt and her pending operation for bowel cancer. I was well aware they did not know she had cancer and therefore I avoided saying anything about it in the first reading, but halfway through the second one, I heard myself relaying the father's advice to them both. He explained the reason for this condition was because she held onto her emotions, and this operation was a wake-up call for her to begin the process of expressing the emotions she had suppressed for most of her life. This situation was just another lesson the aunt had to learn this lifetime, and they had no need to get upset when visiting her in hospital as all would be well. I desperately searched for an explanation for my outburst, apologising profusely to them both. The more I apologised, the more information flowed from me. I finished the reading and as I led them to the door, I attempted to downplay the information I had shared with them.

Later that day I gave a reading to Simon, a young man in his mid-20s. His mother and sister had been to see me previously, so he had decided to come with regard to a relationship he was struggling with. Halfway through the reading, I heard myself telling him about a friend of his who would have a car accident in the very near future, and that it was important for him to tell his friend that the injuries he would sustain from the accident were only temporary, not permanent. "Horrors", I thought, "here we go again!" But instead of allowing my own personality to come in and play it down, as I had with the sisters, I moved onto the next stage of the session. Throughout the rest of the reading, I never saw or felt the accident again.

On seeing him out, I apologised for my prediction about his friend. As I watched him walk down my driveway I questioned what I had shared with him, becoming aware of how I beat myself up for what wrong I may have done. This was an old pattern of mine from way back. Over the next week I thought of my Saturday afternoon clients frequently and the following Sunday I received a phone call from Simon. Apparently, the night before, a friend of his, a rugby player, had been in a car accident and had suffered injuries to his legs, and the doctors were unable to tell him if the damage was temporary or not. He told me he had shared my insights with his friend's family. I thought, "My God! What if I am wrong?" I prayed I was right.

Six weeks later I opened my front door to see Simon and his friend standing there, and I was told the friend had been cleared by the doctor and that he could start rugby again the next season. I was so relieved to hear the news, especially when they told me it was my prediction that had kept the family positive over the past six weeks. I personally believe it was the power of all their thoughts that had assisted in his healing. The family needed to understand the power of positive thought so as to use this skill in other areas of their lives. The young rugby player was able to use the same energy he put into his rugby to gain a promotion in his career. There is always a reason for every situation we create, and it is up to each individual to see the messages and opportunities these situations give us. On realising this I then understood why I had shared this prediction in my reading.

I also heard from the two sisters, and yes, they were visiting their aunt in hospital. She had undergone radical surgery for bowel cancer, but the prognosis was not as bad as had previously been feared. The aunt took this experience as a wake-up call and began the process of expressing the emotions she had held within. I guess my predictions saved these women from unnecessary heartache. They shared with me how they had spoken to their parents while waiting for their aunt to come out of surgery, feeling very connected to them because of the conversation they had had during their sessions with me. This whole experience set them on the path of spiritual enlightenment and subsequently they frequently spoke to loved ones who had passed over. These two situations confirmed to me that it was not for me to censor anything but to say it as I heard and saw it during a session.

Never too late to learn
While there were clients who came for information about their future, there were also a number seeking spiritual understanding and learning. One of my most memorable

clients was Irene, a woman in her mid-60s. Within the first 15 minutes of the reading, I knew beyond any doubt that Irene had terminal stomach cancer. I excused myself from the room on the pretext of needing a glass of water, and while I was in the kitchen I received the message that she was aware of her condition. Within minutes of resuming the reading, I heard myself referring to her future. She then explained that her friends had been to see me, but her own purpose for coming was for me to talk to her about life after death. I had apparently picked up deceased relatives of her friends and because of this she felt I might be able to assist her in accepting the inevitable.

I put my cards away, sat back in my seat and answered her questions with assistance from the spiritual realms. I had to be so mindful of listening exactly to what was being told to me, because the spiritual realms' answers are always at the questioner's level of understanding. This was Irene's first experience at conversing with the spiritual realms and it was important she understood what was being conveyed to her, otherwise our time together would be pointless. It was an interesting experience for me and one I had never encountered before.

After I had answered all her questions she said she hoped my answers were correct. I waited a moment, before picking up her mother, who was waiting patiently to confirm, through me, her presence within the spiritual realms. As a result of this confirmation, we agreed that she would visit me again whenever she felt the need. I recollect that I saw her every three or four weeks, during which time we talked in great depth of the experiences she would have after passing on.

Irene never asked to know about the lessons she had chosen

for this lifetime. It was almost as though, emotionally, she had left this lifetime already. There were times she worried she might be wasting my time, but as I explained to her, our time together was also a healing time for me in regards to my own mother's passing.

Three months after our first meeting, one of her daughters turned up on my doorstep, furious that I was filling her mother's head with lies and nonsense about life after death, accusing me of taking advantage of a dying woman. I chose not to involve myself in an argument with her and thanked her for calling around. Irene was full of remorse when the daughter informed her of our confrontation, but I assured her I was not offended for I understood her daughter's concerns. It was at that point I shared with her my parents' visitations to me. A couple of weeks later she shared this with her daughter, promising to do the same for her, but it fell on deaf ears.

Irene spent her last month in a hospice. I must confess I visited her only once; I was too affected by the energy in the building. I would now know how to protect myself, but at the time I did not. Irene visited me shortly after she passed on, although I never heard from her daughter again. I believe there are a number of reasons for this; either she was too embarrassed because of our confrontation, or perhaps she never felt Irene around her, or maybe she found someone else to explain life after death; I hope so.

Clients of all ages would turn up at my front door and they would come for a variety of reasons. I remember on one occasion a taxi pulling up in my driveway. As I opened the door, I watched the taxi driver assist an elderly woman on two sticks as she made her way towards me. I showed her into my room and I could not help but wonder about the reason for her visit. Her name was Mavis and she was '96-years-young', to quote her own words. Mavis had heard about me through the church she attended and believed I might be able to assist her with some spiritual learning before she passed on; but first she wanted a reading to judge how good I was! In those days, I began my readings by studying the client's palm. It was the first time I'd had the opportunity of reading a palm of that age. As always, I began with the shape of the palm, fingers and thumb and then moved onto her lifeline.

Mavis had begun this lifetime in the north of England, at the end of the 19th Century. She had come to New Zealand with her father and mother to begin a new life in 1913, shortly before the outbreak of World War I. She subsequently married a Kiwi farmer from Southland, and after three miscarriages gave birth to a son in the early 1920s. Her son married in his 20s and just a year into the marriage, became a father of twin boys. Sadly, soon after the birth, her son contracted tuberculosis and died within three years. Her husband died of a heart attack three months after her son's death, some said of a broken heart. Mavis turned to her faith in order to assist in her grief and in doing so began to learn and understand about the process of life and death. She was convinced beyond doubt that her husband and son had remained around her in spirit and so over the years she had had many conversations with them both, especially about running the farm. On their advice she leased the farm out until the twin boys were of age and able to take over the reins. Mavis became the great grandmother of five boys, one of whom she was convinced was her son reincarnated. I neither confirmed nor denied this, nor did she ask me to.

Once we had completed the palm reading, I explained that in the second half of the session I would use a set of tarot cards and we would look at four spreads – three months, one year, two years, followed by a quick spread to cross-credit all that I had already predicted for her. I was amused when she asked me if I considered it a waste of time looking two years ahead; then ended with "Had I seen a man in her cards?" She had a twinkle in her eyes as she spoke, a look I would become familiar with in the months to come. Being polite, I said of course not. Her quick reply was "Good!", as she intended to stay on Earth as long as it took to learn all her lessons on love, because she had no intentions of coming back for unlearned lessons, nor did she want to be taken off-course by another relationship. She was adamant that in her next visit to Earth, she wanted to choose a new set of lessons.

Because of this she asked me if she could come back every month so I could help her to become aware of any unlearned lessons and gain a deeper understanding of the purpose of life. Mavis went into great depth as she described the loving relationship she'd had with her husband. He had loved life and was very demonstrative with his feelings, whereas she was more reserved. Their son was as demonstrative as his father and Mavis believed the two of them were more advanced than she in the understanding of love. She was desperate to understand the power of love this lifetime so she would be with them in her next life. On the first Tuesday of every month Mavis arrived by taxi, and we spoke at great length about the various lessons she felt she had chosen to learn this lifetime.

Two years later, at Christmas, I was invited to her home for a Christmas drink, which I mistakenly thought would be afternoon tea. I arrived at her home with some muffins, only to be instructed to carry out a tray she had already prepared in the kitchen. On entering her kitchen, I saw on the tray a bottle of gin, tonic water and freshly cut lemons. I was told to carry the tray over the road to the seat that overlooked the ocean. I questioned whether it was right to sit in a public place drinking gin, to which Mavis replied "If I can't do that at 98 years of age, to hell with it!"

Halfway through our first drink, Mavis told me she would not be coming to see me anymore, as she believed she had learnt her lessons as 'Mavis' and it was now time for her to join her late husband. She told me her husband would have turned 100 years old on 1 January and that she had decided to join him as a birthday surprise. We both laughed, but needless to say Mavis, true to her word, passed away in the early hours on the first day of that following year. Even now, I wonder who was the pupil and who was the teacher within our relationship. Perhaps we were both pupils and life was, and still is, the teacher.

Our life is our own
Forgiveness is, and always will be, a vital concept in our lives. We are taught to forgive others because it's what is expected of us, and therefore, what we are meant to do. The strange thing is there is nothing to forgive others for; in essence it is to forgive ourselves for having created the situation in our lives in the first place. When one has mastered the art of self-forgiveness there is no need to forgive others. If you feel you have to, then you are not taking responsibility and you are merely blaming others for how you feel. In doing so you are avoiding an opportunity for self-forgiveness. I believe that when you forgive yourself, you are simply forgiving your own erroneous perceptions and beliefs which are not focused on love.

I remember an elderly gentleman coming to see me for the

sole purpose of obtaining some spiritual enlightenment. He was 82 years old and for most of his married life was a consumer of excessive alcohol. People around him were constantly telling him the damage his drinking was doing to his wife and two sons. He had never declared himself an alcoholic, nor had he attended AA meetings. He had supported his family financially, yet he had spent most of his life with a glass in his right hand. He retired at 60 and his sons had left home to get on with their own lives.

Within two years his wife was diagnosed with Parkinson's disease, a shock which prompted him to give up the bottle. Many people told him his wife had developed the condition because he was now under her feet. Whatever the reason, his guilt weighed heavily on his shoulders and he vowed to himself and to his family that he would do whatever it took to make his wife's life more peaceful and harmonious. For the last 20 years he had dedicated himself to looking after her and tending to all her needs.

By the time he arrived on my doorstep, his wife was bedridden and because of his age the health sector had stepped in with nursing assistance to give him some respite. His purpose in coming was for me to assist him in forgiving himself for what he had done to his wife. He believed, and was constantly reminded of the fact that it was all his fault; therefore, he was convinced beyond doubt that he was the cause of her condition. He had a strong faith in the spirit world and he believed I could be the channel for him to hear how bad he had been. He was so scared of dying and being faced with his day of judgment with God.

He struggled with my idea that his wife, by her own choice, had remained in the marriage when she could have left at any time had she truly wanted to. Instead she had chosen to be the martyr and proclaim "Look what you are doing to me!" I told him I considered it was this victim mentality that had created the condition within her body. He struggled profoundly with my explanation and argued passionately as he expressed his feelings of guilt. Now, I am not condoning his behaviour or actions for one moment, but ultimately one must take responsibility for where one finds oneself in the physical world.

There are no innocent victims, for we all have choices and his wife had chosen to stay with him. I explained how it was the lack of self-love within the two of them that held the relationship together. They mirrored this lack back to each other. If he had connected with, and enhanced, this self-love he would never have abused himself as he had done with alcohol. Likewise, if his wife had been able to connect with her self-love, she would never have stayed in the marriage. The bottom line was that it was no one's fault, just two souls expressing a loss of connection with the love that lay within each of them.

Therefore, his first step was to understand and practise self-forgiveness. He needed to forgive himself for not knowing how to connect to his own self-love. This idea took many a month for him to grasp. The only reason he kept coming back to see me was that I had told him on his first visit that he would never drink again and he needed constant encouragement and confirmation that this indeed would be so. As the weeks went by I noted how much stronger his emotional state had become. I watched as he connected to his self-love by taking responsibility for his feelings. In doing so, he began to forgive himself. This in turn gave his wife the opportunity to do the same for herself. In time, he came to understand he was not there to make his wife happy.

It was interesting to note how his wife's health slipped, as she tried, but failed, to continue manipulating his emotions by using guilt and other methods of emotional blackmail. Thus she chose to pass onto other realms, leaving him free to complete his healing process. It took him a further 18 months and then he passed away happy having achieved his goal. Sadly, achievement was not a feeling he'd ever been familiar with in the past. He was such a lovely man and I felt privileged to have spent time with him.

Putting your life on the line
One of the earliest readings I can remember was for a young girl called Sasha, who came to see me as a present for her 18th birthday. I love doing readings for young people because there are so many possibilities for them and not too many disappointments. We sat down in my room and off I went. Her family life was not that great but I had seen a lot worse. She was one of three girls, the middle one, not terribly close to her parents, but then they were not the type that you would want to be close to! She got on okay with both sisters, even though the three of them had gone their own ways. Closeness was not high on their list and neither was expressing love. She was a fairly intelligent individual, working in the hospitality industry and doing some part-time study at the local polytechnic.

I clearly saw heaps of opportunities and possibilities available for her, but I kept on being told that it would be another decade before she would embrace them. I pointed out her potentials and possibilities, but privately I was concerned about how long it was going to be before she could begin using them. As I lifted my head to look into her eyes, I got it. Whamo! She was pregnant and furthermore she had planned her pregnancy. She had been seeing this man in his 30s; he was good-looking, intelligent, and single and had no children. Neither of them had any intention of having a steady relationship, let alone marriage, but she saw him as a good candidate to be the father of her child; she wanted nothing from him apart from a baby.

I was flabbergasted and my old personality kicked into gear at full throttle. I could feel the moral outrage building up inside me. It was time to excuse myself for a glass of water and gather myself together; I knew I had to separate myself from this individual. Before going back into my room, I fell into spirit rather than personality mode. In spirit, I'm never judgemental; I see everything just as it is. While I was in spirit, I saw her reasoning. You see, she so desperately wanted to be loved and to love, and she believed that having a baby would fulfil both these needs.

Her family were angry and critical of her, but she seemed insulated from this because she was just so happy to be pregnant. I continued with the reading, convinced she would study psychology at university and go on to specialise in a particular field; but she seemed uninterested. She said she did not care what she did as long as she had love with her child. As I watched her walk away down my front path, I felt she would have preferred a lipstick for a birthday present, rather than a session with me. When I flipped back into personality mode I felt great sadness for her, yet in spirit I felt the utter contentment she was feeling.

Fourteen years later, this same female arrived back on my doorstep. She had brought her daughter up alone, having no contact with the father, by mutual agreement, and had experienced a deep and loving relationship with her. She sincerely believed she had grown immensely through this experience and had gone on to find a loving partner and marital happiness. By the time she visited me again she was married to a wonderful man and studying at university with the intention of becoming a child psychologist. She informed me she had believed she needed a child to feel safe enough to love unconditionally, before trusting herself to love a partner. Wow! I was suddenly full of admiration for this individual. She had done it her way and just because it may not have been society's way, it did not make it wrong.

Sasha had known from an early age that she had never witnessed the kind of love she somehow knew existed. What's more, she was brave enough to admit it to herself and draw up a plan which gave her the opportunity to experience loving someone unconditionally. How many individuals can admit to themselves they have no idea what love is and then put their life on the line to find it? Talk about having the courage of your convictions! I knew I was looking at a very brave and courageous individual and that being a clairvoyant does not give me the right to judge the actions of others. My experience with Sasha showed me once again how important it was for clairvoyants to come from their spirit and not their personality during readings.

What! No answer?

Sometimes as a reader I was unable to get an answer to a client's question. In the beginning I used to feel frustrated that the answers were not there. Through experience I now realise I was only given what was meant to be passed on at that particular moment- as these next two stories show.

In my second year of readings, a woman called Linda came

to see me. I picked up her fiancé very clearly, but knew they would never get married. I had no idea why this was so, although I knew they would have one child between them. They went on and planned their wedding but postponed it after she got pregnant, because she was having a terrible time with morning sickness. When she was four months pregnant she visited me again and I predicted a son. Even though I felt she would never marry the father, I refrained from mentioning this again during the second reading. I had no idea why I didn't, although I did predict changes in his employment.

Shortly after the birth of her son, she rang to tell me they were moving over to the West Coast and that her fiancé had joined the crew of a fishing boat operating out of Cobden, where he grew up. Six months later, she arrived on my doorstep in a fairly depressed state. The relationship was not going well as her fiancé spent many nights down at the local hotel with his work colleagues. She wanted to know if that was the reason I had predicted in the first reading they would never marry. I still could not get the answer to this question. I tried to explain this to her as honestly as I could, and I said how baffled I was that I could not hear a clear answer.

Apparently they argued a lot and various friends and family suggested she leave him. My advice to her was that the decision was hers and no one else had the right to decide for her. I suggested more communication and for her to look inside herself to see what her lessons were in this relationship. There is a universal law that says 'how you treat yourself is how others will treat you'. Instead of blaming your partner for how you feel, it is more important to see what they reflect back to you; in essence, how you treat yourself. As the conversation continued, she could see that he was doing to her what she did to herself. I always knew he loved her very deeply as his soul was giving her an opportunity to learn something about herself. His disregard for her feelings was exactly how she had treated herself all her life and this subconscious pattern went back to her childhood. As we examined different aspects of her life, Linda saw how this habit had been reflected in most of her relationships and that her fiancé was giving her an opportunity to change this aspect within herself.

She left, determined to master these conflicts in the various relationships she had with her immediate family and friends. She became a lot stronger, stopped regarding herself as a doormat and refused to compromise herself for anyone. About six months later, her fiancé came back from a fishing trip to tell her that he had decided to leave the crew for good after one more trip. He admitted he had been inconsiderate and had treated her rather badly and intended to change his attitude. She was so excited. They talked again about marriage and while he was away on his last trip, she set about planning a small wedding.

Linda rang to invite me to their wedding, but although I didn't say anything, I still felt uneasy. However, I was not prepared for the phone call, a few days later, with the news that he had drowned at sea in a freak accident. It took me a while to overcome my emotions and connect within, but I finally realised that, had all the events not happened in the way that they did, my client would never have learnt the lesson of self-respect her fiancé had so lovingly given her.

Linda moved to the North Island and through people she met became very involved in spiritual groups. The last I heard from her she had become a spiritual guidance counsellor and life coach, calling on her late fiancé for assistance when required.

Clairvoyant mayhem

Jenni was a woman in her late 30s, who came to see me because she feared her boyfriend had some secret life apart from her. She wanted to know what he was up to! Did he have another girlfriend? Was there a wife somewhere? Often, when they were together, he would receive a call on his cell phone and shortly afterwards make some feeble excuse to leave. He told her he was an insurance agent and that this was why he needed to work late into the evenings. Their relationship was great apart from all these mysterious departures at such short notice!

I gave her a standard reading about what her future held for her and what was ahead for her two teenage sons. I then mentioned a problem, which was to do with her boyfriend, though I couldn't get too much detail on it. I knew this trouble would occur in the very near future and that it concerned a man from Australia. The more I tried to obtain details the less I got, but I knew she must warn him about this other man. I assured her there was no other woman involved in his life. I continued on with the reading, adding that she could trust this man and if she did, a marriage would be possible.

About four months later, Steve, a male client in his early 40s, arrived for a session with me. He felt rather familiar, although I knew I had not seen him before in the physical sense.

Within minutes of beginning the reading I knew this chap was trained to kill with his bare hands; he held a black belt in two forms of martial arts. I asked him what he did for a living and, before he answered, I mentioned the name of his girlfriend who had been to see me. I added that I didn't believe he was an insurance agent. By the way he observed me I knew his skill in observation was an important aspect of his career.

His eyes never left me and before he could answer, I heard myself telling him he was an undercover detective. Then the penny dropped for me . . . I can never remember what I have said in a previous reading. As I sat opposite this undercover detective, I thought "Oh dear, what did I pick up that perhaps I shouldn't have?" Intuitively I should have known all would be well, but at that stage of my development I was still somewhat inexperienced.

I started apologising for any problems I may have caused, to which he replied that he had actually wanted to meet me in person to thank me for indirectly saving his life. Apparently after his girlfriend had been to see me, the two of them had a huge argument about him dashing off after yet another late night call, and she had given him an ultimatum that if he left he was no longer welcome back. He left out of duty to his colleagues, but a week later she went around to his home with the tape of her reading, wanting him to fill in the gaps that I couldn't. After listening to the tape he made various phone calls, which assisted in forestalling the disaster I had predicted and helped his colleagues bring a criminal investigation to a successful conclusion.

Of course his main concern was where I had got the information, which was highly confidential, although it would have seemed like garbled nonsense to anyone who didn't know about his situation. My only explanation was that he was being looked after by spirit. He did not disclose any details, nor did I want to know, but I was pleased a resolution had occurred.

Suffice to say, within a year he had left his previous employment and started a private investigation company with another individual, married his girlfriend and lived a fairly settled life. After this experience, I was approached by the Police Department for information on various cases, though really it was not an area I enjoyed because of the negative actions and involvement with criminals it entailed. I find enlightening and uplifting clients far more rewarding.

God moves in mysterious ways

There is a well-known saying that 'God moves in mysterious ways'. There was an incident with a male client who came to see me after listening to a taped session I had had with his girlfriend. He was convinced we must have known each other in order for me to say so much about his personality, although he did admit he could not remember me. His conclusion was that he had known a lot of girls in his time and so must have forgotten me. The fact that I stated I had never met him, let alone gone out with him, fell on deaf ears.

I proceeded with the reading and found I was able to bring to light circumstances only he would have known about. He fearfully asked me where I was getting the information. I spent time explaining that everything we do and think remains in our energy field and I was merely reading it back to him. Very soon this poor fellow was struck with guilt about his actions towards females. I explained the importance of forgiving ourselves for actions we may have taken against others, as guilt leads us nowhere. In fact, we cannot harm others; it is their response to our actions that harm them; we can only harm ourselves. However, if our actions are unintentional, then the impulse behind them is different than if we are motivated by a desire for revenge.

I tried to explain how one doesn't know what one does not know and that his best move was to honour what he has learnt about himself through the experience. For his own sake he had to let go of any guilt, regrets or what-if's, for they would lead him nowhere.

About an hour into the reading, an old oak frame on the wall just outside my room crashed to the floor, breaking the glass that sat inside it. My client's face was one of sheer fright. He was convinced it was his grandmother coming back to haunt him for his attitude to females. He grabbed his jacket and, though I tried to calm him down, he was determined to exit the house.

I heard from his girlfriend a few weeks later how he had mended his ways and dropped his macho attitude towards his female friends. There is a universal law that says 'there are never any accidents or coincidences', so it was interesting the string on the back of that frame chose that particular time to break. I believe he was led to me to hear and experience what was needed in order for him to change, for his own sake.

Who's that in my ear?
It used to amuse me when people rang up for a booking and asked if I was 'Angela, the clairvoyant'. I had never really seen myself as that. In fact I have never really put a label on myself as such. I guess it's because I detest labels and boxing people into certain roles or niches; something carried on from teenage years perhaps. So I used to laugh and say, "Yes, I have been called that". For me, my clairvoyance was a gift or an ability to see images in my mind of events, people in the past, or scenes of the future for the client sitting there in front of me. I would explain what I saw as best I could in human terms, which meant translating the visions into words.

After a couple of years, I began to hear names being spoken, but interestingly it was never the same voice I heard. I assumed these voices were telling me someone of that name was either thinking of me or perhaps asking themselves whether they should ring me for an appointment. To be honest, I really didn't know what I was meant to do with these voices and so I tended to dismiss them. I confess I was too busy seeing the images before me to pay too much attention to what I was hearing. However, the more I tried to ignore them the more frequent the voices became.

One Saturday afternoon, I was seeing two women who choose to sit in on each other's readings. Saturday was the end of the week for me and these women had the last appointments for the day. I finished the first woman's reading and started on the second one. I was about 10 minutes into the reading when I became aware of hearing the name 'Nichols' over and over again. My energy was finely focused and I stubbornly resisted the voice as usual, but as I began describing my client's two sons to her, the voice kept repeating 'Nichols'. Out of curiosity, I asked her if one of her son's was called Nicholas. I can still see her face as she laughed and said "We would hardly have done that, given our surname is Nichols. Nicholas Nichols, neither of them would have liked that." Ah! A revelation . . . those voices I had heard all this while related to the client sitting in front of me. It was at that moment I realised my clairaudience had kicked in fairly strongly.

Without batting an eyelid, I thought to myself if I could hear her married surname then surely I could hear her maiden name. As I gazed out the window, I asked for clarity on the maiden name, but of course the more I tried to hear the voice the less I heard. Instead, I surrendered and let it go. In doing so, the stronger part of me, the clairvoyance, kicked in and I saw in my mind's eye a picture of meat in gravy with raisins. So I guessed – stew; Stewart! That must be it. I turned back to her and asked, with much confidence I might add, if her maiden name had been Stewart. She looked quite oddly at me as she exclaimed "No, it was Curry." I burst out laughing, which unfortunately upset her somewhat as she exclaimed she couldn't see anything funny in that and proceeded to spell the name out as Currie. I didn't bother explaining but continued with the reading.

Suffice it to say, I made friends with the reoccurring voices as I added the gift of clairaudience to my abilities. The more I listened and shared what I heard with clients, the stronger and more frequent the voices became. Sometimes the names meant nothing to clients at the time of the readings, but often they would ring me later and say they had just recently met someone with that name. The stronger the gift became, the more I could explain what effect the named person would have on my client's journey through life.

With clairaudience, I found that sometimes I didn't quite get the name right. For example, Julia could sometimes be Julie; Carol and Karen were another two names I would mix up. Of course, some names can be both surnames and Christian names, like Stewart and Martin. Collins can be confused with Colin and William with Williams or Williamson. Nevertheless, I had fun playing with my new-found gift. As always a sense of humour was vital. Of course, when Asians came for a reading I had great difficulty in pronouncing the names I was hearing. It became a good exercise for me to focus my attention on what the spirit realms were telling me. Sometimes my interpretation of the names caused great laughter.

Some of the Asian clients could not speak or understand a word of English and would come with an interpreter. I must confess I found these readings intriguing because I could just tune in, say what I saw and felt without interruption or any interaction from them as they couldn't understand me; and because of their beliefs they were usually very open to read. There were some who brought a tape recorder with them and a note saying that a friend would translate the reading for them from the tape.

I found those readings fascinating as they gave me great opportunities to strengthen my gift as a clairvoyant. It also proved the information I received from the other realms was beyond the human barriers of culture and race and that my ability to read someone who could not speak my language, nor me theirs, was made possible by extending my inner senses into the energy field that surrounds each person.

3

Heaven help us Now

- ♥ She did, he did!
- ♥ Please take control of my life!
- ♥ Family patterns – love 'em or hate 'em!
- ♥ Woe is me!
- ♥ Moving from woe to go!
- ♥ I can't do that because . . .
- ♥ Beware of free-riders!
- ♥ What one does to oneself!
- ♥ Seek and you will find!
- ♥ Heaven will help you now!

Heaven help us Now

During my sessions with clients and course participants, I would explain the importance of taking full responsibility for all circumstances, events and situations that happened in their lives. This was what I called their outer world, in which they could never blame others or circumstances for the negative experiences that happened to them. I believe individuals are responsible for how they perceive the world around them. If they choose to see problems in their lives it is important for them to understand and take responsibility for having created them.

This happens from within the self; the situation is literally being viewed through one's own feelings. Now, to some people this may seem rather harsh or unfair, but the truth is that in learning and understanding the way of the spirit, it is necessary for them to realise they are pure spirit, and that spirit comes from within the self; it is who they are. The only way to feel close to the spirit is to go within.

When people accept that they choose to react to every situation in their outer world, that the associated feelings are a direct result of choice, only then can they begin to become powerful from within. Individuals become powerless when they blame someone else, or outside events, for what happens in their lives. I would explain in my sessions that this does not mean they have to be a martyr, but that it is vital people speak up for themselves.

When communicating with those around them I recommended they come from their heart and never diminish their spirit by allowing others to walk over them. I emphasised how important it was never to allow themselves to be controlled by others, whoever the others may be. Becoming a target for abuse, blame and a whole host of other negativity would never happen in the first place if the subconscious was not bedevilled by low self-esteem and low self-worth.

The key to achieving spiritual growth is to go deep within the self (the subconscious memory banks) and rearrange negative thoughts and feelings with affirmations and meditations. If the subconscious is comfortable with failure because of low self-esteem, then that is what will be delivered in its outer (conscious) world. Therefore, it is crucial to practise loving thoughts, to trust and appreciate others and to refuse to judge or condemn people. When this is done consistently it will manifest positive thoughts and actions in return.

She did, he did!

I had a number of female clients who came to see me in the late 1980s and early 1990s wanting to know about their financial future. Their husbands had played the sharemarket in the 1980s and were financially ruined in the crash of 1987. These women had believed they would be financially secure for life. Their children had attended private schools and their homes had been mortgaged to the hilt to free up capital for investment purposes. As their problems unfolded, many had been forced to sell their homes in mortgagee sales. Their children were back in state-run schools, the spending sprees had come to an abrupt halt and many marriages had folded under the pressure.

Many of the women who came to me were by this time living as solo parents in rented accommodation. They harboured immense feelings of anger and resentment against their former husbands. Because of this I decided to put together a course focusing mainly on forgiveness and acceptance of the present situation. I endeavoured to provide them with the tools to create and discover gifts within themselves which would introduce change in their lives. Their first lesson was to forgive themselves for being in that financial predicament. They were then urged to forgive their husbands and eventually to cease blaming them for the situation they had found themselves in. I offered these women tools to discover the messages and lessons being presented to them. Each woman's story was different yet there was a common thread that ran through them all.

With a little self-honesty, many of them were able to see the pattern that had been part of their marriages and in some cases this pattern had been seeded way back in childhood. Some were very angry that their husbands had been greedy enough to risk the security of their home and family. However, with self-honesty, many saw that they had also been prone to this reckless greed. Others recognised what little responsibility they had shown by not keeping themselves informed of their financial situation; instead they had blindly trusted their husband's every decision to maintain the illusion of 'keeping up with the Jones's.' As each woman gradually reviewed her situation, she saw she was as much to blame as her husband for the situation she found herself in.

I repeatedly emphasised how important it was for them to take responsibility for where they found themselves and to put a plan into action for getting where they wanted to be in the future. Many were forced to see that it was time to revaluate and decide on a career in order to become financially independent. Did they go back to the occupation they were in before having children or did they map out another direction for themselves? It was also time to look within for the reasons why they had chosen to relinquish their power and financial independence in the first place.

It was important for them to understand that to create massive change in their outer circumstances, it was vital to make dramatic changes within. Some got it, some didn't. The main stumbling block was forgiving the husband and changing the belief that it was all the husband's fault. I tried many times to explain that holding onto this belief blocked any advance. Sometimes my words fell on deaf ears, which I now realise simply meant the individual was not quite ready to take responsibility for her choices. Some didn't hear or didn't want to hear what I was saying. I also learnt that some people need to hurt badly before deciding to change and, if they don't hear the message, they are not hurting enough.

Please take control of my life!
As a clairvoyant, I am only able to pick up what the clients in front of me have created for themselves and sometimes I found there was very little to say when clients had created nothing in their life. I recall in my early days of readings that when a client like this came to see me, I would struggle to find anything. I would look deeper and think the reason I was unable to see anything was my lack of ability. Other times I believed it was my lack of experience that was blocking my information channel; (that was a family pattern I carried – to

blame myself when things didn't work out).

On one particular occasion, the more I searched within, the more empty plates I saw in my mind's eye. By listening to my higher self, I realised the reason the plates were empty was that the client was not creating anything significant for me to see or pick up on. In time, whenever I was shown empty plates, I would ask clients what their thoughts were on their future and if they had any plans for themselves. Every time the answer would be the same – they had no idea what they wanted and assumed I would be able to tell them what would happen to them. Horrors against horrors! Reading between the lines, what they were really saying was "Please take control of my life because I don't know what I want." Nine times out of ten they were oblivious to the universal law that we create our own future.

That is when I would start the process of brainstorming with them. I would begin by describing to them their personality traits and I would emphasise their natural abilities and talents, which they had brought in from past lives. Some would look at me oddly and proclaim that I was flattering them. Others would admit to having these talents or abilities, but I was the first one to mention it to them. Then they would explain that they couldn't possibly say anything to their friends and family in case they would be considered conceited.

That is a common trap many individuals fall into – believing that someone else's opinion about what they can and cannot do contains more truth than their belief in themselves. Individuals like these have allowed others throughout their lives to direct or advise them on the path they should or must take. The only one who truly knows what is right is the individual concerned. That is why it is so important to connect with your own master within, listen to the direction given and align yourself with it. Then and only then will you be on your right pathway.

I always encouraged clients to make a promise to themselves, to devote their time and energy to connecting with their inner world. In doing so, they will be in control of their life. When you experience and feel this inner power you will never ever hand it over to others. You will never find solutions to your problems outside yourself because all problems are self-created and so the answers can only lie within. Therefore, we attract to us what we ourselves believe. The more we dwell on something, the quicker we see it manifesting in our existence. If you want to know the nature of your thought patterns, become aware of the circumstances within your life. What you do as a career, your state of health, your relationship with others, the car you drive and condition of your home are merely photographs of your inner thoughts. Your outer world is a mirror of your inner world.

The fantastic thing is that you can change anything outside yourself by merely changing your inner world. You are in control. Your thoughts become more powerful when you feed them with your emotions. It is so important to let go of negative feelings and emotions, because these create negative circumstances. When you cease to dwell on negative circumstances they will miraculously leave you. I tell my clients that in order to move forward in their lives, they must make changes by focusing their energy on what they want to become, not merely what they believe themselves to be. When you do this, you enter a new realm of consciousness. When your inner being truly believes you are there, then your outer world will reflect this back to you. This is another aspect of the Universal Law of Reflections.

I recall doing a reading for Dianne, a woman in her late 50s. Her husband had left her for another woman 15 years earlier and her three children had married and were living their own lives. Two of them were overseas and the third one lived in another city in New Zealand and she complained she rarely saw them. Throughout the session she constantly told me how lonely and boring her life was. After checking into her energy field, I had to agree. There was no excitement for her, nor did she create any.

Everything was too much of an effort and because nobody cared, neither did she. Though I tried to uplift her and find a thread of optimism to expand on, I found nothing. Before long, I realised nothing I could say was going to make a scrap of difference. Life to her was one huge struggle. Halfway through the reading, I heard myself say "Do you enjoy being so negative?" I recall to this day, her facial expression as she looked up at me and said "I'm supposed to be negative, I'm a Capricorn! All the books I have ever read on astrology say Capricorns are negative and pessimistic, so how can I be anything else?" Ye Gods, I thought. If that wasn't confirmation of the saying, 'You are what you believe' then I didn't know what was!

One might think it was a waste of time for someone like her to come and see me. Many might ask themselves, "Why would she bother?" But the fact of the matter is that she did make that effort. Somehow, her higher self led her personality into my room for whatever reason and hopefully, from our meeting, she received what the inner realms saw would be valuable for her soul's growth and evolution. Often it is the transference of energy between two individuals that is important and not necessarily the words that are spoken. Our personalities don't often see the wider picture but our souls certainly do.

Whenever I experience a situation like that I feel blessed to be chosen as the channel by that particular soul. It is not important to know the reason or even the logic behind our encounters with another individual. Our purpose is just to trust that the Universe assists in placing us at the right place, at the right time, with the right people, to experience the right lesson we need at that moment. That is all we need to know or understand.

Family patterns – love 'em or hate 'em.
Family patterns have a tendency to control our lives if we let them. By practising self-observation, we enable ourselves to see the circumstances we constantly create in our lives. It is our belief patterns that create our outer circumstances. The norm is to blame this person or that person for painful or negative circumstances and events. However, if we are able to step back and practise the art of self-awareness, we soon realise these events are put in our path as an opportunity to learn a valuable lesson, one which we have previously chosen to master during this lifetime.

Marie and Karen were two sisters who came to visit me on a regular basis. Throughout their childhood, when anything went wrong, their parents, instead of practising self-responsibility, became experts in passing the buck. Marie became expert at defending herself against other people's behavior, whereas Karen lived her life as a victim for others to blame. The constant tape running in her mind said "It must have been my fault, I'm so terribly sorry." Karen could spot a problem arising long before it materialised and sure enough, as she expected, it manifested right in front of her. She chose a husband who constantly blamed her for everything. Her son copied the husband in his behavior and attitude both towards her and her daughter, Caroline. As the years went by, Caroline became a carbon copy of her mother.

At work, Karen was the victim of endless mishaps and consequently felt the world was against her. Her longest employment in any one job was seven months. She constantly suffered throat problems like laryngitis and swollen glands. In my view, the root cause of these problems was the frustration she carried and the feelings she was unable to express. Over time I learnt more about the family; Caroline had had her tonsils removed because she suffered constantly with tonsillitis. Karen had had the same operation as a teenager. Now, many would say that tonsillitis can be a hereditary condition, but in my opinion it is the emotional and behavioral patterns we inherit that determine the illnesses and diseases we manifest in our physical bodies.

While her sister decided to become a victim, Marie chose to go in the opposite direction, spending all her energy on constantly defending and justifying herself. Marie threw herself into her career but every job ended in an ugly termination. She was constantly seeking legal advice for what she believed was unfair dismissal; always blaming her employers because she saw them as controllers like her parents. Marie had a tape running in her head that went like this: "How dare they do this to me? Who do they think they are? No one is going to treat me like that."

Marie decided to attend our workshops on self-development and eventually obtained a career position she had always dreamed of. Within six months the same old problem surfaced again. This time though, instead of defending or justifying herself, she decided to accept the situation gracefully. They could chose to believe what they liked about her; that was their business; but it was not her truth and it had nothing to do with her abilities or capabilities or lack thereof. Marie had finally found self-love and self-worth; and she knew this belief was all that mattered.

On surrendering her habitual pattern of behaviour, a miracle occurred – the firm offered her a generous severance package providing she left the company without a hassle. By accepting these terms, she was able to complete her law degree in financial comfort. On completing it she stepped into a law firm, which gave opportunities for her to stand up in court, day after day, defending and justifying her various clients' cases to her heart's content. She was superb at this; and, at the same time, in changing her attitude within, she allowed others to be themselves. Miracles kept occurring in her life and she no longer attracted people who were opinionated or critical into her energy field. She had learnt one of the biggest emotional lessons her soul had chosen to learn in this incarnation.

Marie's story illustrates one of the major universal laws we teach in our courses; 'Whatever anyone says or does to you has nothing to do with you and everything to do with them' – they are defining themselves. How you react to what they do or say has everything to do with you and nothing to do with them. When you apply this to your relationships with others, you notice a feeling of freedom as you excuse yourself from another person's reality.

Woe is me!
I believe the number of opportunities and possibilities that are available are only limited by the scope of your imagination. There are no reasons for failure for they are just excuses

many individuals use to justify their victim mentality. In fact, you can never fail. You are merely ignoring the messages from the Universe. If you do ignore the messages, you create further opportunities, courtesy of the Universe, until that particular lesson is learned.

A common trait of victims is the belief that one does not deserve the best that life can offer. With so much available in the area of self-development in the form of seminars, courses and books, I have never worked out why so many people still choose to live mediocre lives in victim-consciousness. I believe it is partly through fear, partly through not knowing how to get out of a situation and being engulfed by feelings of helplessness and hopelessness. Perhaps these people prefer to kid themselves that they are happy and fulfilled; maybe they enjoy the sympathy they get from being victims. Of course, it is everyone's right to choose how they wish to live their life. But it is important not to judge other people's choices.

Gill, a woman in her 50s, came to see me the first year I began doing readings. She'd married in her early 20s and even 30 years later still felt privileged to have married into a well-to-do, highly respected family, although her husband abused her and was known throughout town as an alcoholic in denial. By the time she saw me, their three sons had moved out of home to attend university in other cities throughout New Zealand, to get away from the family situation and more specifically their father's drinking problem. None of them had any time for their father because of the physical, mental and emotional abuse he meted out to the family and particularly his wife.

The two reasons she gave herself for staying in her marriage, were that it gave her sons a father – she herself came from a single parent family – and that she enjoyed the status and income her marriage gave her. By the time the last son left for university, she had added a third reason for staying – she was too old to be on her own. She complained constantly to friends and family about the terrible time her husband gave her, yet she still chose to remain with him.

She came every six months to see me, but nothing much altered because she had made no decisions to change. Her friends, who also came to see me, believed she loved being her husband's victim, but I struggled to accept that as her truth. The hatred she felt and expressed towards him was somewhat alarming and I often thought about how this attitude would be affecting her health. On one occasion while I was giving her a reading, I received intuitively a very clear message that Gill would be filled with deep regret when her husband died. I became very conscious of this message and thought, "There is no way I can say that." But, as spirit moves in mysterious ways, next minute I heard the words fall out of my mouth with me adding "Of course, I'm not predicting his death you know." I remember very clearly her facial expression as she declared she would be dancing with joy on his grave and no way would she have any regrets. I moved on very quickly to another topic after this outburst.

It was a few months after this that I received a phone call from her saying her husband had dropped dead of a heart attack just before his 60th birthday. Would you believe it! He had left considerable debts around the country, mortgaged the house to the limit, had no savings and had cashed in all the insurance policies. She was more or less penniless, sitting in a house waiting for the mortgagee sale date. If only she had left earlier, but as spirit would say "If we want to be a victim then we will create circumstances to ensure we will be!"

I believe that as human beings, one of the biggest mistakes we make, and continue to make, is the act of compromising ourselves when it comes to relationships. I'm not just referring to male/female relationships, for it occurs in parent/child, sibling/sibling relationship as well as in work-place relationships. Some individuals believe they have to compromise themselves for the good of those around them. I believe no one has the power to force another into compromising. It is all done voluntarily. My advice to anyone who wishes to listen is that, if you ever feel you have to compromise yourself in any shape or form, are expected to, or need to for whatever reason, take a deep breath, turn and quickly walk away. In fact, run! Nothing and no one is worth you changing who you are.

The next step is to strengthen your self-respect, self-worth and self-love by reading books on the subject, going on courses or talking to someone who specialises in assisting individuals in this area. Constantly examine your level of self-esteem and keep moving away with great speed from all compromising situations. Once you express this to the Universe, you will notice that those who are now around you, whom you have attracted towards you, would never expect you to compromise yourself; nor would they compromise themselves in their own relationships. This is the Universal Law of Attraction – everyone mingles with those of similar thoughts. We are taught through our schooling and within society how to compromise. My advice is to unlearn this aspect of life as quickly as you are able to.

Some individuals who are stuck in victim-consciousness

enjoy coming to see someone like me, because they are searching for sympathy and an opportunity to vent their anger and frustration at what they believe the world has dished out to them. Some even blame others for the damage in their lives. These individuals are somewhat horrified at my reaction to their beliefs, especially when I inform them rather bluntly that everything in their lives is self-created. All they have to do is to stop blaming and take responsibility for their choices. So many sit back and wait for life to happen to them or for them, creating nothing; then they wonder why nothing happens in their lives. Some are fearful of change because they're scared of making mistakes. If they could only understand that you can never make a mistake, and that if something doesn't work out as planned you have a choice to try something else.

Victim-type personalities are scared of being in control. They choose to lose control over events, situations and circumstances in their lives and allow themselves to be ruled by fate. Most people hold onto what little they have mainly because they feel too insignificant to embrace life to the fullest and realise their true destiny.

Not all my clients walk away happy and uplifted. The main reason for this, I believe, is that they didn't hear what they wanted to hear. Some people come to see someone like me because they believe their life to be in tatters and that somehow I will be able to wave a magic wand I have stashed away in a cupboard to make everything turn out the way they want it to be. They believe I will be able to do this without them having to put in any effort at all. Sorry, but the Universe does not work that way. There are some fortune-tellers who pride themselves on the fact that they can solve people's woes with a few spells and magic rituals, but all they are doing is conning you. It is a universal law that "There is no one and nothing outside you that can create change or make your life different, apart from your self."

A true clairvoyant can only pick up what you have created for yourself in the future. Yet at the same time they are able to see what you could create if you were to put your mind to it. That is why some clients will say "Oh, she told me what I have been thinking about," or, "I knew that already and it was great to have it confirmed." Whatever you have created by your thoughts, beliefs and emotions are in your energy field. You carry them around with you every moment of every day. No one put them there but you. This is the other aspect of taking full responsibility for your thoughts, words and actions.

With these thoughts lodged in your energy field, you will attract to you circumstances and people who can take these creations to the next stage and then the next and the next. It is that simple. Hence the principle: "Be continually mindful and aware of your every thought, word and emotion."

Unfortunately, there are some individuals who give their power away to things and people, totally oblivious to what they are doing. They believe that it is the government, the economy or society that does it, but they can't even describe who 'they' are. What is more alarming is that these individuals truly believe that someone else has power and control over them. They say they don't like the control the government, economy or society has over them, but it is their own beliefs that control the power they give away. It is that absurd. More times than not, these individuals believe it is sheer good luck or chance that good things happen to them. This belief reeks of what I refer to as victim-consciousness.

Nick came to see me hoping I could tell him what to do career-wise. His 24 years had been spent listening to others' opinions on what he should and should not do, could and could not do, must and must not do. Sound familiar? He was an only child and his father had been killed when he was just two years old. He had no contact with his father's family, who lived in Holland. His parents had come to New Zealand from Holland two years before he was born and his mother was estranged from her Catholic parents because she had married a protestant. Her parents had since died and Nick's mother was his only family.

Because of her own fears, his mother decided everything for him; there was not one area in his life where his mother didn't make the decisions. On tuning into Nick, I was shown why he had chosen such a difficult beginning in this life. In the past, lifetime after lifetime, he had chosen co-dependency rather than independence. He had chosen to be born into families who were emotionally entangled, making it easy to survive in a co-dependent manner but it had stunted the growth and evolution of his soul.

For this lifetime, in order to learn independence, he had chosen a life stripped of all relationships, bar that of his mother whose own lesson was to learn to allow people the freedom to choose their own paths. For this soul to experience peace, happiness and love he needed to learn independence, strive to free his real self and find the means inside to support himself financially, emotionally physically and mentally.

Now, one could say he had chosen a tough life this time round, yet on exploring his soul's path it was noted he had the tools within to achieve independence. Unfortunately, Nick found it difficult to step forward to this challenge. The easier option, the one he had chosen so many lifetimes before, and thus was familiar with, was to stand back and be supported. His destiny, however, was to get in touch with his inner strength and the power of his own energy vibration. This was a lifetime to re-discover himself and to follow his own direction.

Halfway through the session with him, I asked if he knew who he really was . . . who he believed himself to be. He replied what his mother had repeatedly told him. There is a subtle difference between who you think you are and who others think you are. I asked him again and more of what his mother had said came out. He had absolutely no idea of his own identity and what identity he did have was very weak. Because of this weakness, he was easily influenced and affected by others, believing they knew better than he did.

All his relationships mirrored the relationship he had with his mother. The difficulties he had experienced in his relationships were mainly brought about by his having spent all his energy focusing on the relationships he might or might not have had with various people rather than on the individuals themselves. When I enquired further, you could count on the fingers of one hand the number of friends who had come and gone from his life. He never had more than one friend at a time and more often than not he was on his own.

Nick believed, as his mother had told him, that he was unable to relate to a lot of people, and circumstances in his life confirmed this to him. It was not so much that he couldn't relate to others, but rather that he found it difficult to relate to himself. My advice to Nick was to take time to focus on himself, what he wanted to do and where he wanted to go, without any input from anyone else. I said it was time he began to centre his attention on himself and discover what it was that brought him happiness and fulfilment. Needless to say he left my room rather disgruntled. He was unable to manipulate my emotions in order to fulfil his need for me to give him direction about what to do with his life. Instead, I handed it back to him – his life was his responsibility and the day he realised that would be the day he could begin to create changes for himself. I heard through the grapevine that Nick's visit to me was not his day to begin changing himself.

Moving from woe to go!

Emily was in her early 30s when she came to see me. "Woe is me," was the only way to describe her energy. She had chosen to be a victim all her life and she had held on tightly to the belief everyone was out to attack her. Because of this belief, that is exactly what she experienced. She was classed as dyslexic at school and those around her thought she was stupid. Her parents criticised, judged and attacked her constantly for her stupidity and so she believed her parents when they told her the best thing she could do was to find a rich man and marry him. Thus she focused on marrying someone wealthy and sure enough, that is exactly what happened. Her husband came from a wealthy family and was a high achiever like his father. His mother was a victim, like Emily, and so the cycle repeated itself. Emily constantly received abuse and put-downs from her husband and, because it was what she expected, she accepted it.

As luck would have it, her father-in-law fell in love with another woman and left his wife. Emily's husband followed suit. He told her callously that he was sick of living with a doormat. She cried as she told me this. I attempted to explain how lucky she was to be free of him. He had given her a gift if she could only see it, for now she was free to be the most wonderful person she could possibly be; now she had no husband telling her how hopeless she was. I told her I would not insult her by feeling sorry for her because of what he had done to her. How could I? Emily had received exactly what she herself had created.

I explained that, while I felt compassion for her, she had been given an opportunity to develop herself. If she could accept she was responsible for creating everything in her life, she could then take back her power and create anything she wanted in her life. Whether it was positive or negative would be up to her. The first step was to change the beliefs and attitudes she held about herself, for these had created and perpetuated the situation she lived in. Everyone and everything around her treated her the way she treated herself, with abuse and lack of respect. Emily had received what she had believed she deserved.

Over the next six months, Emily focused on changing the way she saw herself by reading books on self-esteem, self-worth and self-love. One morning she rang terribly excited, saying she intended to do a design and arts course at the local polytechnic. Often people who are dyslexic are excellent in creative areas. I am pleased to report Emily completed her three-year course with a B grade and moved forward into her career. She became very selective about her relationships and promised herself she would never compromise for anyone or anything ever again.

Emily was a good example of why it is important to become aware of how you treat yourself. Once she had done this she was able to attract people who treated her as she wanted to be treated. It is all very logical when you think about it. How you feel about yourself determines how you behave, what type of person you are attracted to and who is attracted to you. You are who you believe you are. If you believe you deserve respect and love, then you attract people and circumstances that confirm this belief. In doing this, you create scenarios that enhance this belief.

I remember a friend of mine who constantly complained about the people in her life, who were always promising to do certain things for her, but hardly ever followed through. Also, although she had had a number of serious relationships, none of these men had ever asked her to marry him. When she sat back and analysed her relationships, she realised that none of the men had really been committed to her, and that it mirrored just how little she was committed to herself. She would often promise herself a holiday but never follow through by making any arrangements. She would decide to go somewhere, but forego her plans when a friend wanted her to do something else. She often spoke of buying herself a two-seater sports car but never quite got round to it. She constantly talked about those extra three or four kilos she was always meaning to take off by changing her diet and doing some exercise, but never got round to that either.

Once she took a good, hard look at herself and decided to change, suddenly friends began to follow through on their promises and those that didn't dropped away. The universal law of 'how you treat yourself is how others will treat you' is very powerful. The more you practise self-honesty and integrity in your dealings with others and yourself, the more you will grow.

I can't do that because . . .
I have had many a client come to see me for help to point them in the right direction. There were a number of married

women in their 30s and 40s who gave up their careers to have children; and once they were settled in school, the women took part-time jobs either to help pay the bills, or to get out of the house, or to have extra money for holidays. Sadly their jobs were not what they really wanted to do. Were they happy? No. Did they feel fulfilled? No. Were they prepared to do anything about it? Nine times out of ten the answer was also no. Do you know why? Although their individual reasons varied, most of them believed they had to be available if the family needed them. A decade or more later, they found themselves in hospital, where they met others like themselves with similar health problems.

I believe the root cause of these problems stemmed from years of pent up frustration and anger brought about by constantly putting others before themselves. After all, your physical body is a reflection of your emotional and mental state. Now, if you choose to bash your head against a brick wall, go for it and don't let anyone stop you. But do not complain about the pain you are inflicting on yourself, because no one wants to know and neither do they really care. This is a hard, but very true fact of life. I am not saying every mother should branch out into a full-blown career, with exacting hours, as soon as their kids are in school, but, if you do decide to work, make sure the job is something that interests you; then grab it with both hands and enjoy every moment.

Beware of free-riders!
This leads me to another group of individuals out there – the ones who fly on other people's coat-tails. The only reason why someone is sitting on your coat-tail is because you have allowed them to do so, either because you feel sorry for them or you believe they have something to offer you. Check your coat-tails frequently and, if anyone is there, the kindest thing

you can do for both of you is to shove them off. If you find you are the one being shoved, take a long hard look at yourself.

Sometimes coat-tail flyers are there quite innocently, enjoying the ride because they do not know where else to be. If this is the case for you, then ask yourself "Am I doing what I really want to? Is this where my passion lies? What percentage of my passion is in this venture?" Sometimes we might work with someone to establish a business and there will come a time to move on. When this happens you will have learnt all there is to learn for your soul's growth. If you find yourself in this position, take time to ask the Universe to confirm whether you are on the path that has your name written on it; then sit back and wait for the signposts. If there are other things for you to do, the Universe will only too willingly guide you in the right direction, so that you realise your full potential in this lifetime.

What one does to oneself!

One of the most horrendous stories I encountered in all my time of readings was that of a Chinese male from Singapore, who came to see me because he believed I could give him some 'inside' information on his past relationship. He was so consumed with hatred and revenge because the woman had left him that he spent every waking moment plotting ways to get back at her for the pain she had caused him. I was astounded when he offered an unlimited amount of money for me to cast spells on this poor woman as punishment for leaving him.

Instead, I spoke of forgiveness and love of the self but, unfortunately, my words fell on deaf ears. I heard from other sources that over time he suffered a lingering and painful death from cancer. What we do to ourselves! I once read somewhere that evil thrives where there is an absence of love. I don't believe anyone is fated to become evil; but it can happen when someone strays from the path of love, becomes blinded by negativity and can no longer connect with the soul.

Seek and you will find

The workings of the Universe never ceased to amaze me. In my readings, I would often find a common thread between clients booked within a short space of each other. For example, if a hairdresser came to see me, within a week I would end up with half a dozen of them. Mind you, hairdressers, beauticians and other practitioners were great for my business because they would recommend me to their clients.

To illustrate this, I will share with you the time an older woman came to see me after her daughter had already been. She was a madam at a well-known massage parlour and within days I had numerous bookings from local prostitutes. I had never had anything to do with women in this line of work; and to be perfectly honest I was strongly critical of their chosen career. When they pulled up in their cars outside, I could pick them as prostitutes by the energy field around them.

I had spend the first hour studying and reading their palms; and each of these women had lines which indicated sexual abuse at an early age – mostly before they were five years old. These lines carried on throughout their childhood often continuing into the present. Sexual abuse was part and parcel of their lives. As the readings unfolded, it was interesting to learn that this was one of the main reasons why these women came to see me. They didn't want to hear about their future; they wanted to heal their past. They all carried so much deep-seated emotional pain from their experiences.

Eventually, I decided to get a group of them together every Wednesday morning for eight weeks. Most of them already knew each other or of each other. I put together a course on forgiveness, healing the past, self-love, self-worth and self-respect. The stories that were told and the depth of their pain were almost unimaginable. I continued for almost two years; a new batch of women every two months. A large percentage of them ultimately changed their profession and moved out of town to start a new life; this was one of my greatest successes. But there was always another batch of sexually abused females waiting in the wings to fill the vacant spaces in this industry, once my course participants had moved on.

It took me a long time to fully understand the reasons why; yet I knew that we all choose what we choose in order to learn what we need as a soul to grow and evolve. From my encounter with this group I also grew and as a result I now view this profession rather differently. This was one of their many gifts to me.

Another group I attracted as clients were women between their late 40s and mid-70s, who had given birth out of wedlock and had adopted their babies out. They came to see if I could 'pick up' the birth and if this were so, if I could share any information on the life this child may have experienced. They all wanted to know if their children would contact them, especially since the law had changed to allow adopted children contact with their birth mothers. The shame and the pain these women carried was very deep, yet their need to know about their children far outweighed their feelings. They all wanted reassurance that they had done the right and best thing for their child.

Of course none of them confided in me outright. Instead they waited for me to broach the emotional subject of their youthful indiscretions and the babies they had been forced to give up. Always the tears flowed. I suggested putting a course together for a group of them to assist in healing their past, but their shame was too great. Furthermore, what would they say to their husbands? (To this day I've never been able to come to any conclusion over which is the easier option for a woman – adoption, solo-parenting or abortion.)

I remember one particular client who told me she was on a bus, travelling home from the city, when she overheard a woman telling a friend about her visit with me. The woman was expressing the relief she had felt after talking to me about being forced to adopt out her child in her late teens. My client waited on the bus until the two friends disembarked. Then she followed the woman to ask her for my name and number.

As she sat in my room telling her story, she cried as she remembered the familiar feeling of shame she had felt as she approached this woman. The birth of her first child – the result of being raped at 16 – had been laced with so much pain and heartache. She had been born into a farming family and had four brothers. In her family the prevailing attitude had been that one brought most things on oneself, so one should shoulder the blame and get on with it. Thus she had told no one of the incident, until of course, she found herself to be pregnant. Because of her silence, her family had not believed her story of rape. Shamed and outraged, her parents had forced her to leave the district in disgrace, and for the rest of her life her siblings had shunned her.

I can to this day remember the look in her eyes, as she told me she had had to wait 54 years for someone to believe her story – and a stranger at that. She had never married and therefore had no one else to consider, apart from herself, if she did connect with her lost daughter. She often came to see me in her quest to heal this trauma and by the end of six months she had taken the veto off her file.

Within four weeks of doing so her daughter contacted her and welcomed her into her family unit. The adopted parents had both passed on many years before. My client found herself to be a great grandmother. As the years went by she took an active role in the upbringing of her three great grandchildren.

These last two stories illustrate the desire within to heal. I believe we all want this, yet often we have no idea where to go for assistance or we feel we don't deserve to be happy. Never, in all my time of seeing clients, did I ever make judgments about what they should or should not have done in any situation. I consider it is no one's right to pass judgment on another. People often go to a clairvoyant because they feel 'stuck' in their lives and so I would voice what was possible and offer ideas on how to make these possibilities a reality. Unfortunately, there are individuals who struggle to understand that they are entitled to all the Universe has to offer. They would leave a session uplifted and inspired, but then the old habitual feeling of not being good enough would reassert itself.

Sure enough we create what we believe, so within days, sometimes weeks, these people would create mayhem in their lives as confirmation they were not worthy of the possibilities available to them. Then, back they would come to see me with the latest installment. I did not care what they had done to create the situation; all I was interested in was assisting them out of their own way. I once read a saying 'My life is one big obstacle race with me as the chief obstacle'.

Heaven will help you now

Assistance from above is never too far away; you just have to ask and the Universe will oblige by giving you signposts or directions. You may have a revelation, during the day, or the message may come through other people. You do not have to be extremely intuitive to receive these messages, just aware. I believe every one of us is tuned into our intuitive voice; and the more you ask for confirmation the louder the voice becomes. It is always in the gaps that one can hear the messages; all we have to do is listen. I tend to use it as a game because I find the Universe responds with humour.

Let me tell you a personal story to illustrate this point. About 10 years ago, a friend of mine who was intuitively gifted, was coming around home for a coffee. On opening the front door to her, she informed me that the daphne plant in my front garden was screaming out to her that it needed cold tea leaves to survive. We had our coffee and on leaving, she advised me not to forget to put tea leaves around my daphne bush as it would die if I didn't. I laughed to myself, took a look at it, decided it looked healthy enough and did nothing.

A couple of days later she rang to tell me the daphne had come to her in her dreams, telling her I had scoffed at her advice. At the end of our conversation she suggested I ask the Universe whether she was correct or not. Anything for a game with the Universe! So with a certain degree of scepticism, I asked the Universe to enlighten me on the health of the daphne bush. I continued on with my day and later in the afternoon I was standing in front of two elderly women at the checkout in the local supermarket, when I overhead one of them say how much healthier her daphne bush was now that she had been feeding it cold tea leaves. It could not come clearer than that. So, my daphne was fed tea leaves and my friend won the bet. The daphne bush coming to her in her dreams was something I declined to try and prove either way. As I said earlier, all you have to do is ask, listen and be ready to receive.

4

You can Run but you can't Hide

♥ *What on earth happened?*

♥ *Wake up to our karmic returns*

♥ *It's a done deal*

♥ *A gift or a mishap*

♥ *Self-honesty erases Karma*

♥ *The balancing act of Karma*

♥ *Anyone for a game of blame?*

♥ *Now what . . . the choice is yours!*

♥ *Hey, don't I know you?*

You can Run but you can't Hide

We are all governed by universal laws whether we are aware of them or not; even when we do not know they exist. Everything that happens is governed by these laws and there are no exceptions. Over the centuries man and society have created their own laws and, as history has shown, these laws have changed as society's beliefs and customs have changed. While society's laws may evolve, universal laws remain constant.

The universal law I find the most intriguing is the Law of Karma, often referred to as the Law of Cause and Effect. My interpretation of this law is that whatever you do, whatever you say and whatever you think will be returned to you. You have a choice of what to say, think, do and feel every moment of your life. This is the gift or opportunity the Law of Karma grants you. If you come from your heart and act with love, compassion and understanding then you will attract and experience this in return.

I sincerely believe that if everyone understood this law the world would be completely different. The Law of Karma is in action each moment of every day.

I remember when a friend of mine wished to open a business with three other people. The landlord of the premises dearly wanted them as tenants and so decided to reduce the rent to ensure they took over the lease. Now, some may say they were lucky, but I say there was no luck involved. Instead I saw it as an example of good karma. The four individuals created favourable circumstances for themselves by exuding good intentions. Within a week, the landlord was offered a higher rent for another property he owned, which made up the monetary difference.

Tithing is another means of creating good karma; in giving financial aid, you in turn will receive assistance when you need it. If everyone was aware that what they sent out they would receive back, no doubt they would be far more generous and charitable in thought and deed.

In the last chapter, I related the story of the woman who came to see me to find out about her daughter whom she had adopted out. She had focused on loving herself before contacting her daughter so that her energy field radiated this love outwards. Because her intentions were full of love, the Law of Karma created the situation whereby she could be a part of her daughter's family.

The story of Emily – also in the previous chapter – illustrated different karmic situations. She radiated negative energy towards her husband in meekly accepting the role of doormat, which in turn was mirrored by her husband's treatment of her. In choosing to change her inner world and thus reclaiming her power, she created a career for herself and then a relationship in which she commanded respect.

When we give with love and with no expectations of receiving anything in return, we are creating positive karma for ourselves. The more pure, true, loving and compassionate your energy is, the more it will 'boomerang' back to you. What you feel in your heart is exactly what comes back to you. Sometimes we give our love to people knowing it will not be returned. This is okay. It is still important to share your love with them, for in doing so you are offering them and yourself a choice to witness unconditional love.

Whatever you give out will come back to you, although not necessarily from the same source. It is not necessary for you to keep the score of karmic deeds; but trust me, the Universe always does. Someone somewhere will return the favour, courtesy of the Law of Karma.

Negative energy is sent and returned the same way. If anger radiates from you, as it returns, it creates even more anger. Why? To help you make a decision to erase the anger within. How? Simply by letting the anger go and choosing to feel a more positive emotion. In doing this, you transform the karmic return in the future.

Karmic debts can be balanced very quickly by forgiveness of the self, thus changing the energy field within. Remember the elderly gentleman in Chapter Two, 'Don't shoot the Messenger'? Once he understood the importance of forgiving himself, his energy field changed and he was able to balance his karmic debt. Your intentions and choices change when you come from a place of love, understanding and compassion. If a negative situation continues to occur then you have missed part of the gift. Ask the Universe for a sign to assist you. Take each lesson one at a time.

What on earth happened?

During my time of working as a clairvoyant, two of the most frequent comments I heard were: "I must have been really bad in my past lives to experience the suffering I have endured in this lifetime" . . . "I want to know what I did in my last lifetime that has created my bad karma". I cannot emphasise enough that karma is not something to fear and certainly not a punishment for doing wrong. Karma comes from love not from fear, because it is a part of the universal energy that contains love in its purest form. The Universe never judges. All it does is return to you whatever energy you send out.

If there's been an absence of love in your actions or behaviour in past lifetimes, then you will be given another opportunity to take a more enlightened and loving stance. No one and no thing causes anything to happen to you, except yourself. It is simply your energy, creating an opportunity for you to become aware of what you are doing 'for or against' yourself; so that you have the choice to make a different decision. I refer to this process as karmic returns – an opportunity for an individual to learn what it feels like to view the world with love.

Wake up to your karmic returns

In my experience, negative karmic returns occur through lack of self-awareness. These offer you the opportunity to understand that you are solely responsible for the energy you project. Your actions are simply a reflection of your intentions. Emotionally charged thoughts or intentions will produce strong returns. Whenever you sour your energy with negative emotions like aggression, or anger, as a result of fear, you will create angry, aggressive situations around you. Karmic returns, including negative ones, are sent with love in order for you to learn something about yourself. That is why

I treasure the karmic returns I receive, for these experiences give me an opportunity to recognise, and then heal, any disorders buried deep within my subconscious.

A few years ago, I had a neighbour who bought an established coffee shop with some redundancy money he had received. Within three months he had deliberately created situations which caused the five employees, all middle-aged women, to leave so that he could hire teenage staff and thus only have to pay youth rates. This was his first karmic mistake. He then decided to reduce the ingredients that went into the food and drinks, while at the same time increasing his prices. His intention was to rip-off his customers, though he didn't see it quite like that. When your intention is to take from or cheat others, then you will be taken from or discover that someone is cheating you. That's karma.

Within 12 months his home had been burgled four times and he had been involved in three car accidents. His insurance policy premiums went up accordingly. I sat back and watched, knowing that the Universal Law of Karma was in action. It was not the ex-staff or the customers who burgled his home. He created his own karmic return and a burglar robbed him of his possessions. Because he did not understand what he was creating, it happened another three times. After the third car accident he called to ask me what was happening to him. I did try to explain but unfortunately he didn't understand the philosophy. He shifted house shortly afterwards claiming the neighbourhood was unsafe. I don't know for sure whether he was burgled at his new address; but like us all, he takes his karma with him.

It's a done deal
It doesn't matter whether your karma is good or bad. What

is important is how you deal with the next opportunity your karmic returns offer you. Sadly, some continue to walk away from love and thus create further disasters and chaos for themselves. I sincerely believe that ultimately they will embrace the love that is available to them, and that it is no one's right to judge those who are in a state of unawareness. Because we don't know everything about our past lives, we don't know what karma we have already created. The good news is that it really doesn't matter. What does matter is how we use the frequent opportunities offered to us. What also matters is to live in the present moment and deal with what is happening now.

We are constantly creating karma for ourselves and we have the choice to decide right now whether it be positive or negative. It is how we behave, think, see and feel at any given moment that determines the outcome. My advice to you is not to waste time rueing the decisions made in the past. Because you can't change them, but you can make choices in the present moment that will shape your future.

A gift or a mishap
You have the choice to see a karmic return as a gift or a mishap. Your choice determines whether you have created or erased karma for yourself. Bear in mind that when you take from others all the time, you have no time to give. When you argue all the time, you have no time to love. It is your choice which side of the spectrum you come from. Do not be fooled into thinking you can run and hide from your karmic returns. Believe me when I say that you cannot. Why? Because you carry your energy around with you, constantly radiating it out from yourself, and what you sow, so shall you reap. Your karma is part of you; it is your responsibility whether it is positive or negative.

Therefore, karma is not something to fear. How can it be, when you created it for yourself purely as an opportunity to grow? Learn to recognise any negative energy within you. Let go of emotions that no longer serve you and do not, whatever you do, avoid or attempt to hide from your karma. If you try to reject or push it away, you are only rejecting yourself.

As I stated earlier, in my opinion karma comes from a love space as it offers us gifts for our soul's growth. Karma is part of the universal energy, so how can it be harmful to us? The only way we are harmed is if we inflict damage on ourselves. No universal law is negative. Individuals who have learnt how to create wealth for themselves draw it towards themselves. That is karma. Those who have learnt to create chaos and mayhem in their lives, draw this to themselves. That is also karma. It is the same energy only laced with different emotions or intentions. When you come from your heartspace you create positive karma. When you move away from this heart space you may create negative karma for yourself.

Self-honesty erases Karma
One of the most valuable gifts we can give ourselves in regards to the Law of Karma is to always be honest and true to ourselves. Self-honesty involves looking at the feelings surrounding our actions, thoughts and words. That is, become aware of what we are doing and then to examine why we do what we do. What are the intentions behinds our actions? Are we coming from a space of love or alternatively reacting to a fear we are holding onto? If it is the latter, take a few moments to reflect then adjust your state of mind so that you come from your heart.

It is so important to be honest with yourself, to find your own truth; in doing so you connect to the power that resides within. I am not referring to a power that controls people or situations outside yourself; I am referring to the energy of your own truth. When you feel this power, your confidence and self-esteem is strengthened and everything outside yourself loses control over you. Therefore, in practising self-honesty you automatically express your self-assurance; others pick it up and respect you accordingly. If you respect yourself others will too.

Many of us live as others wish us to live and if you find yourself in this position it means you have simply surrendered your power to someone else. In doing so, you have defrauded yourself. Dishonesty towards oneself is often present in people who want others to think they are perfect. But not everyone will see you as perfect for we each have our individual degree of truth.

A person who practises self-honesty will always be honest with you. They will often be blunt or direct but they will also allow you to hold your own truth; they will not browbeat you into accepting their ideas and opinions. Self-honesty also enables you to grow and evolve, as it is the key to welcoming change in all aspects of your life. For example, if you change your beliefs within, then your outer world will automatically change too. It is a universal law that your beliefs create your outer reality.

There is a well-known saying that 'you can fool some of the people some of the time, but not all of the people all of the time'. You can fool yourself, but you can never fool the Universe. The Universe keeps the score even if you do not. 'If you lie to yourself you will be lied to' . . . That is another universal law, the Law of Reflection.

There are some individuals who believe they can, and will, get away with harming others. Sometimes it seems that they do walk away without a scratch on them; but underneath, hidden, the Universe keeps the score. No one escapes from their karmic returns, though they might come from an unexpected source. This applies to both positive and negative reactions. Every thought and action has its effect and, while some individuals can convince themselves and others of their innocence, the Universe is never fooled. There is much truth in the saying that 'you can run but you can never hide'. Sometimes individuals may have to wait until the next lifetime to reap what they have sown, be it positive or negative, but it will happen eventually.

If you find yourself in a situation where you feel you need to lie to yourself about your actions or behaviour, ask yourself why. There could be a number of reasons, but certainly it will result from a pattern of behaviour in your past. You often see this in parent-child relationships, where the parents will make all the excuses under the sun for their child's actions or behaviour. They can't bear to think their child is less then perfect, or that others may be judging their parenting skills.

I had a female client who lied to herself about her husband's behaviour and actions because she couldn't bear to see that he was less than perfect. When her husband fell out with others, and this was a frequent occurrence, she would always take his side, blaming the others for causing her husband's outbursts; altering the scenario to create the illusion of her husband being right. In this way she could justify her loyalty to him. Unfortunately, she could not see the negative karma she was creating for herself through her constant self-deception, and the situation would continue to repeat itself until she learnt to take responsibility for her actions and words.

The balancing act of karma

The Law of Karma will always balance out a situation. When we feel we have been slighted by someone, we may harbour thoughts of revenge and want to pay that person back for the pain we feel he or she has inflicted on us. I am sorry to say, acts of revenge create more bad tidings for the maligned individual. Eventually, you will always receive back what you have given. Therefore, it is important to forgive the person you perceive as having wronged you and most importantly, forgive yourself for having created the situation that attracted this reaction in the first place. When you do not let go of a negative situation, you only create negative energies within your world, which, in time, will produce other negative scenarios.

I recall a client of mine who always looked for ways to get back at different individuals whom he perceived as having wronged him. These scenarios were constant throughout his life because he always hit back. He constantly retorted "Just wait, I'll get him" as he waited for the moment when he could avenge himself. No sooner had he punched his foe when a similar situation would arise with another individual. Eventually he began to understand the universal Law of Karma and in doing so, he made different choices about how to respond to these scenarios. He chose to ignore the actions of others and instead blessed them for the insights they showed him about himself. Over time the conflicts ceased and he realised he had learned one of his major karmic lessons.

Another example was a female client who came to see me after she had separated from her husband. During their marriage her husband had borrowed $100,000 from her parents for a business venture. He was always promising to pay it back but unfortunately the business went into receivership and the money was lost. This was an example of her husband's belief that he didn't deserve good things to happen for him; it was one of his soul lessons to transcend in this lifetime.

Her husband experienced bouts of depression because of the business failure. As a result of this and a number of other problems they decided to separate. Twelve months later the husband won a first division prize in Lotto of almost $400,000. He was fantastic at creating money, but holding onto it was another story. Instead of offering to repay his former parents-in-law the money he had borrowed, he ventured into another business.

Within 18 months he had lost this new business and he was declared bankrupt. Seven years later this man continues to repeat similar scenarios in regards to money, although he hasn't been fortunate enough to win a big lotto prize again. He chooses to blame everything and everyone for his predicament rather than taking responsibility for his thoughts and actions.

His wife, on the other hand, viewed the business failure as an opportunity to learn more about herself. She became aware of how she compromised herself in their marriage. She realised how much she relied on her husband to do the right thing rather than acting on her own intuition. She knew in her heart the business was doomed from the beginning. She had agreed to borrow the money from her parents because she felt her husband needed financial assistance and justified it to herself because he had never received any assistance from his own parents. Also, she was too scared of the confrontation with her husband that would have ensued had she refused her parents' assistance.

After the separation she set about confronting her fears, and in doing so learnt that any abundance around her reflected the level she accepted and expected in her life. Within months she availed herself of an opportunity to enter the real estate industry and became one of its top sales people. Instead of resenting her husband, she forgave both him and herself for the actions they had both taken. She chose to see the gift this experience had given her. Now that she understands the Law of Abundance, she will never repeat this experience of losing money again. It is a universal law that everything that happens through you has the potential to strengthen you and it is your responsibility to search for that gift.

Everyone is given an opportunity to get back onto the right path, but sometimes the habitual pattern is too strong or the individual cannot see the gift or opportunity that the experience offers them. Sadly, because of this they tend to stay on the road of self-destruction.

Anyone for a game of blame
Unfortunately, at an early age we are taught how to blame others or circumstances when something negative happens in our life, when in actual fact, it is ourselves who have created the situation through negative thought or deed. Every choice, thought and decision we make in the present has an effect upon what is to come. What we choose determines happiness or further problems. Simply put, our choices in the present moment create our future. We all reap what we sow.

So often I have had clients who have spent most of their sessions with me going into great detail about what somebody has done to them. If they only knew that by blaming, judging, back-stabbing, bad-mouthing or holding negative opinions about others, they are creating karmic mayhem for themselves later on down the track. Eventually they in turn will be back-stabbed and bad-mouthed by someone else. It is vitally important for your own sake to refrain from making negative comments about others, or indeed yourself.

It is also important not to pretend that other people are responsible for your present situation. I would explain this in great detail whenever I felt a client was caught up in this behaviour. Some understood it and I would recommend they followed through by reading some material on karma. Creating karma like this in your life is like banging a dozen nails into your left foot and then shooting a dozen bullets into your right foot. Karma will always come back to you, courtesy of the Universe. Well you did create it in the first place! You can spend as long as you wish blaming circumstances or others for your predicament, but all you are doing is creating another disaster for yourself in the future. It is up to you.

There are no accidents in this world. Everything in your life is there because you created it for the lessons you need to learn. When you understand this, then you will realise that you are not the victim of outer circumstances. You do indeed create your own destiny and everything that happens along its path.

Now what . . . the choice is yours!
We have seen that how you choose to respond or react to the events and situations in your life at any given moment will determine the type and extent of karmic return you create in your future. As I mentioned earlier, your karma is the echo that bounces back to you. If your intention is positive then you will receive positive feedback. Negative karma is usually created because of a lack of self-love and self-worth within. Negative

intentions create negative karma. Positive intentions create positive karma.

This reminds me of a story I heard once about a male in his early 20s, who always found it difficult to walk away from an opportunity to play pranks on people. One evening after consuming some alcohol, which impaired his judgement of the situation, a joke back-fired badly. Realising the extent of his error he walked into a police station to own up. Against the advice of his friends this young man was completely honest about what he had done and said he wanted to rectify the situation. Being spiritually aware, he was conscious of the mayhem he had created and admitted to it; and in doing so he also let it go. In doing this, he neutralised his actions.

Unfortunately the other party was not at all forgiving. He indulged in abusive language, lies and aggressive behaviour, thus creating negative karma for himself. Two weeks later all repercussions were erased for the prankster, whereas the other party experienced verbal and physical abuse from another group of abusive individuals.

When you realise the force of karma, then you become extremely careful with your intentions. My partner, Michael, has his own architectural design practice and was approached two years ago by a group of individuals to design a large project for them. There appeared to be conflicts of interest within the group, who found it difficult to agree amongst themselves on various aspects of the project. Michael witnessed their constant back-stabbing, criticism and deceit. He decided to withdraw from the project just as the concept was submitted for council approval. The approval was granted and another designer was employed. The karmic returns for the group resulted in the project eventually folding, whereas Michael, in letting the project go, received much media publicity for his original design concept. Owing to this publicity and his personal integrity, within a matter of weeks he attracted a variety of larger and more interesting projects.

Hey, don't I know you?

One of the things I discovered along my spiritual path is that people come into your life for a purpose and it is you, and only you, who have created this. That is what I refer to as karmic connections. These relationships offer you an opportunity to grow and evolve your soul; they mirror something back to you about yourself. The more aware you become the clearer you will read these messages. You could liken the people around you as gifts from the Universe – the stronger the interaction you have with them, the stronger the karmic connection you have with them.

These connections will be through your association during past lives and the more intense the message they give you, the more intense the connection and the more soul growth you will both experience. At every moment you are given a choice to grab hold of an opportunity or let it pass you by. The more aware you are, the more likely you will recognise them. It doesn't matter if you do not, for circumstances will occur to create other opportunities for you to learn the lessons necessary for your evolutionary progression along your soul's path.

People in our lives are there to assist us in learning the lessons our soul has chosen. Sometimes they are there to help create the circumstances needed for us to learn. No person is in your life without a reason. They have lessons to learn from you too in order for them to grow. This applies to the most negative or horrendous of situations as well as positive and uplifting events. There are no innocent or chance victims; and, as I mentioned before, there is no such thing as luck. It is the way we respond to these situations that determines whether we have learnt our lesson or whether we need to go through a similar situation until the lesson is learnt.

You may remember in my first chapter, the story of my meeting with Alice from Thailand. A matter of weeks before meeting each other, Alice had had a health scare and, while doctors were convinced surgery was required, Alice felt intuitively she could be healed naturally. I introduced her to a spiritual healer who agreed to treat her and with that Alice embarked on a journey of healing. It involved healing aspects of her personality and emotional body, which, we believed, had caused the condition to occur in the first place.

Within six months this condition disappeared. I met her husband, Seri, on their second trip to Christchurch and I felt an instant recognition. Two months later they invited Michael and me to Phuket in southern Thailand, where we spent four amazing weeks in each other's company. Eighteen months later, through a connection of Alice's, we started our courses in Singapore. A karmic connection existed between the four of us.

Karmic connections are present in every family but some are stronger than others. I believe as souls we choose our parents and earthly circumstances before we arrive here on planet Earth. We do this in order to learn and grow from the challenges and opportunities our family patterns will teach us. Many of these family souls we have known before. Sometimes these connections are amicable and sometimes they are downright challenging. If this is the case, then there is a fantastic opportunity for the growth of all souls involved. I recall a story of a young boy, Scott, whose mother was quite involved in spiritual growth and encouraged his spiritual awareness. A family with a son the same age moved into the neighborhood and attended the same school. Within a short time a strong friendship had developed between these two eight-year-old boys. Scott began playing at his new friend's home after school and on his return home he spoke about the layout of the place – the shape of the stairway, the size of the rooms etc. Scott's mother was mildly concerned as she had endeavoured to teach her children it was people that mattered, not the material wealth surrounding them.

A few days later, after Scott repeated how he felt about his new friend's home, his mother explained to him that the house wasn't important; rather it was the friendship that was of value. The mother was somewhat bemused by her son's expression but thought no more of it, hoping that he understood what she had said. No more was said regarding the house, until she went to collect him one wet afternoon.

As she drove up the driveway she began to appreciate why he was so impressed. She knocked on the door and was led into the hallway and then on into the kitchen. Later, as they drove off down the driveway, Scott asked her how she felt about the house. The mother began to repeat her message – that material things were not important, but yes, it was a beautiful home.

Her son looked confused as he exclaimed "But Mum, I thought when you saw the inside of the home you would remember." "Remember what?" Asked the mother. Scott replied "When we lived in a house like that, with the stairway curved like that one. You know, when we were together before and you were my sister, not my mother. I thought you would recognise it when you saw it." Oh how we forget our spiritual memories the older we become in Earth years.

I believe we are the sum of all our past lives though we may not be consciously aware of it. I truly believe I chose to experience my parents dying before my 30th birthday, so I could learn from the lessons and experiences that situation gave me. I also experienced rejection from my in-laws. However, rejection and loss provided me with the opportunity to become self-reliant and independent; I became stronger. Sometimes I wonder if I would have developed my intuition to the degree that I have had my circumstances been different. I could have chosen to rely on the state as a beneficiary with two small children, but instead I chose to start my clairvoyant practice. I chose to become self-responsible.

Karmically this situation enabled me to be free, although, at times, it may have been easier to have looked on rejection and loss as bad karma. I could have wondered what I had done to deserve it. I could have decided that I must have been bad in a past life, and so on. But I do not believe that was the case. I feel I chose the circumstances to assist me in becoming who I am today, tomorrow and forevermore.

5

I have it but I have it Lost

♥ *How do I love myself?*

♥ *Hey, I think I'm in love with my wife!*

♥ *Mirror, mirror on the wall*

♥ *When love is purely fiction*

♥ *What we resist will always persist*

♥ *Dying for love*

♥ *Make me happy*

♥ *When love is found*

I have it but I have it Lost

For me, the most enjoyable moments of being a clairvoyant was when I would inform clients that everything they needed, they already had within themselves. All they had to do was discover it. The best part of all was explaining the process of connecting to it. Let me explain with a story.

Thomas came to see me after several disastrous relationships. Thomas searched relentlessly for love outside himself, never connecting to the love within. In fact he half-heartedly believed his former wife's claims that he was emotionally cold. Thomas had a great love for nature. He loved plants, gardens and all animals. I recall his face when I asked why he didn't love himself to the same degree. His understanding of love was from an intellectual viewpoint; he constantly analyzed what love should be, rather than feeling it inside. I explained why it was necessary to come from his heart rather than his head. He felt it when he looked at nature and animals, but somehow his emotions cooled when it came to his relationships with people.

Thomas was convinced love was some sort of abstract, idealised concept that didn't really exist outside romance fiction. When I asked about his childhood, he told me his father loved people and his work but he had never expressed any love for him. As for his mother, he felt she had only done what she considered was her duty as a mother, and had not loved him either, or herself for that matter; he couldn't remember ever having been cuddled as a child.

When he was 25, Thomas married a woman who also lacked any experience in expressing love. This is a prime example of the Universal Law of Reflection in action. The couple had three children and Thomas worked hard and long hours to be a good provider, just as his father had done. Not surprisingly, however, the marriage was a disaster – an endless cycle of blame, emotional blackmail, emotional and mental abuse and third-party entanglements. Finally, the marriage came to an end and Thomas spent years searching unsuccessfully for happiness in other relationships.

Thomas agreed to come to our workshops and in time he learnt how to feel the love inside. He learnt to satisfy his own emotional needs by taking time to do the things he enjoyed. In giving to himself, he had more to give to his family and other relationships. He came to understand the principle that in order to love others and receive love in return, one first has to love oneself; and he let go his fear and his destructive thoughts, feelings and actions. In doing this he observed how his life became filled with love and he witnessed things he never thought possible. He finally recognised that the outer world around him was but a reflection of his inner world. Thomas changed from within and entered a relationship where both he and his partner helped each other with their individual challenges.

How do I love myself?
I purposely spent much time explaining self-love, self-respect

and self-worth to my clients. I believe, and have learnt from my experiences of communicating with the other side, that we are all made of love, although it is often submerged by fear, hurt or anger. A question that is frequently asked is "How do I love myself?" The universal truth is that when you love yourself, you automatically put yourself first. In doing this you will realise you are the most important person in your world and that your thoughts, ideas, dreams and desires must take precedence, because only you can ever make them a reality.

The trick is to focus on what you want and then set out to achieve it, provided it does not harm others. Whatever anyone says about you, whether it is positive or negative, must not affect you. If you get upset about what others says about you, it means you value their opinions more than your own, and in so doing you relinquish your power. Ignore their criticisms. Their words say a lot about them and have nothing to do with you. Be aware of your own emotional needs, and take the time to do the activities you enjoy. When we give to ourselves first, we have more to give to our family and relationships. Never sacrifice yourself too much, or you will lose the ability to truly give and receive. If you love yourself, you will be able to love others and the Universe will respond by creating opportunities for you to express it.

How we experience the world depends entirely on how we decide to see the world. Take time to listen to your heart. The more you love yourself, the greater number of loving people you will attract around you. So many individuals chose to focus on what they don't have rather than what they have. The Universal Law of Thought states that what you focus on you strengthen; and if that is envy and resentment, then those emotions in and around you become stronger and the positive aspects become weaker.

When we are in touch with our soul, we automatically experience the power of love within. I advise clients to spend time alone in meditation or contemplation and to have a conversation with their soul. Those who find this difficult usually have a trust issue. However, if or when they do go through this exercise, they begin to trust themselves and likewise the Universe and other people. The more in touch you are with your soul, the more connected you feel to the universal love and wisdom that is available to us all. Think of your soul as your best friend, always wearing a warm smile; in time you will find you are smiling too. The more you practise this, the more you will feel a change in your inner world. In time this change will be reflected in your outer world as well, and your relationships with others will also change. In doing this you are letting your soul shine through and those around you telepathically pick this up.

Whenever you are in an emotional state, ask yourself "Am I acting through love or fear?" If it is the latter, then analyse that fear and walk through it, imagining your soul by your side. The situation will not go away unless you deal with it. Furthermore, no one else can do this for you, though friends can certainly hold your hand. I suggest you think of your soul constantly, and take time to review each day's events and activities from a soulspace. In doing this, your whole perspective on life will change.

Hey, I think I'm in love with my wife!
Family patterns and beliefs can rule our lives and create obstacles if we allow them to. I believe as souls, we choose our parents for we see the opportunities they can give us which will assist us to evolve.

Warren was in his late 30s; he had been brought up in a small country town in Southland, where he'd married a local girl. Both families were happy about the marriage, but in hindsight he realised that, while he loved his wife, he had never been in love with her. He viewed her as his oldest friend, somewhat as a sister. They had two teenage sons and six years prior to seeing me, Warren's company had promoted him and the family had moved to Christchurch. Friends and family saw their relationship as the perfect marriage. Warren's wife was an excellent mother and played the 'corporate wife' to perfection. He spoke of their friends envying their 'perfect relationship'. All was well until his boss, at the age of 48, dropped dead of a heart attack. This prompted Warren to re-examine his life and his marriage. In doing so he suddenly realised he had never been in love. He felt that in his home life he was role-playing.

On coming to see me, he explained he had spent the last two months just watching this perfect family he was part of and realised that he did not really know any of them. He had no idea what subjects either of his children enjoyed at school and, though he greeted his sons' friends warmly when he saw them, he had no idea what they had in common, apart from being the same age. Because his father had left the family home when he was a teenager and because of his religious beliefs on divorce, Warren was fearful of the future. He felt guilty for wanting out, believing he was selfish in wanting to be happy. He was also fearful about being on his own and losing a secure relationship, even though he felt it was loveless.

I took a deep breath before explaining to him that it was not for me or anyone else to tell him whether to leave or not; though I did recommend that he make a conscious effort to connect with his family, before throwing everything away. I suggested that perhaps it was time to stop role-playing and be honest with himself and his family. I added that a family discussion might bring to light how each of the members felt. I also said it was helpful that at least he had not waited until a third party was involved; as that was often the case in similar scenarios I had witnessed. He left feeling slightly better, though somewhat nervous at the prospect of a family 'heart to heart'.

Three months later he called to thank me for our session. There had been many changes, big and small, within the family. He and his sons had joined a trail bike club and spent time every weekend with each other. He reeled off the various names of his sons' friends and also the subjects his two boys enjoyed most at school. After talking to a work colleague, he suggested to his wife that the two of them go out for dinner once a fortnight, just to catch up with each other. At one of these dinners his wife had revealed she had always wanted to be an interior designer. By the time he rang me with the update, she was attending a course at the local high school with the intention of doing full-time tertiary study the following year. His last sentence to me was "Hey, I think I'm in love with my wife!"

Mirror, mirror on the wall.
I believe we are all searching for love. Most of the individuals who came to see me wanted to know either about their existing relationship or how to find one. The way to attract a relationship is to focus on strengthening one's own self. The Law of Attraction is constantly working away in your life. You can only attract someone who is similar to you. Therefore, the key is to clean up your own act by looking within. Discover what you are holding onto that no longer serves you and let

it go. The energy level that vibrates within you is the same level of energy you attract to you. There is much truth in the sayings, 'You are who you mix with' and 'Birds of a feather flock together'. Your energy level is made up of your conscious and subconscious. The key is to become the type of person you want to attract into your life. Recognise your underlying beliefs and behavioural patterns and change them if need be, because those you attract are reflections of yourself. Your inner world is reflected in your outer circumstances and situations. This is the Law of Reflection.

Gregory came to see me out of curiosity. One of his female colleagues had recommended he come along, even though he was pretty sceptical. He had never met anyone like me before, let alone had a reading. He'd married in his early 20s and had four sons. He had worked hard and had become a successful businessman. On first meeting Gregory I noticed he had a certain degree of arrogance and strong opinions on everyone and everything.

Shortly after beginning the reading, I realised Gregory found it difficult to relate to people, mainly because he wouldn't listen to other points of view. The lack of insight and emotional support during a crisis involving one of his sons, had signalled the end of his marriage. His wife announced she wanted a divorce.

Two years later, Gregory was still stunned by his wife's desertion. His comment to me was "What happened? What went wrong? I gave her everything she could possibly want. I prided myself on being a good provider and she wanted for nothing." He must have asked me six times during the two-hour session to explain why she had left him. I noted that not once did he mention love, just the material possessions he had supplied.

When I eventually mentioned love, his response was "We had been married far too long to talk about love. Everyone thinks like that after 20 years of marriage." I asked him if it had been talked about in the first few years of the marriage and his reply was "Well, you didn't talk like that in those days. Everyone was so busy building a successful life for themselves. It was necessary, otherwise you were unable to upgrade your home and lifestyle."

Many would say it was no wonder she left him, and I guess she got tired of him never expressing his love; but when one delved further back into Gregory's childhood, the lack of love he had experienced was obvious. Was that his fault? No. He was merely living as he had been brought up to live; we are all products of our upbringing. It's not until we practise self-awareness that we realise what we are doing to ourselves. Gregory sincerely believed that by providing generously for his wife and children, he had been expressing his love. How the children felt I have no idea but I do know that we all choose our families to learn the lessons our family patterns can teach us.

Within a month of the reading Gregory rang inquiring about our courses. He believed that by attending them, he would come to understand his wife's problems, and in doing so, know how to get her back. Halfway through our 10-week course, Gregory realised he had some work to do on himself and that just maybe, it wasn't entirely his wife's problem after all. The couple did not get back together, but they became the best of friends. Over time Gregory also became more loving and less arrogant and self-opinionated.

The relationships we attract are there to teach us what we need to learn about ourselves. Many individuals will compromise in order to remain in their relationship. I knew a young lady, Sara, who felt rejected by her father because he had abandoned the family when she was only eight years old. For many years she chose males who also rejected her, mainly because she was not true to herself. A relationship where one or both parties are always compromising will never last. It simply cannot, because the Universal Law of Reflection will step in. Perhaps a scenario will be created where there's a third party entanglement, or one of them chooses to leave for some other reason. The subconscious mind will pick up when the other party is not being true to themselves. In Sara's case, her partners mirrored her worst fears – rejection and infidelity – thus giving her an opportunity to learn these soul lessons.

I first met Sara when she was 43, with two teenage sons and many disastrous relationships behind her. Over the time I knew her, she spent a lot of time and energy changing and growing and recognised the pattern in her relationships. She vowed that next time she would be true to herself. After two further brief liaisons, Sara finally married and found happiness.

Every relationship is a reflection of aspects within you. Whatever qualities you like or dislike about another person, you must have them yourself, otherwise you would never recognise them. Learn how to read these reflections so you can recognise aspects of yourself that you wish to enhance or discard.

I had a client, Margaret, who used to visit me on an annual basis around her birthday. She was a woman in her mid-

50s who constantly complained and criticised men. She had lived with two different men before marrying in her mid-20s. Her first two relationships ended because of a third party involvement. In her marriage both she and her husband had constant affairs. Margaret never owned up to having affairs herself, although she was always quick to talk about those of her husband. Finally she met her soul mate, or so she believed, and moved in with him. After his fifth affair she moved out in an attempt to get on with her life.

Over five years, Margaret had affairs with three married men, which caused tears and pain for all involved. Her resentment and bitterness was immense, and as far as she was concerned, the pain and anguish she suffered was always the man's fault. It certainly did not help that her former husband, the father of her children, had found the love of his life and was happily married.

By this stage she had convinced herself that all men were fickle and so she decided to become a lesbian. It wasn't long before Margaret asked her new love, Justine, to move in with her; alas, within three months, Justine was having an affair with another woman.

I did not hear from Margaret for almost three years; but after another two similar scenarios she turned up for a session. She said she wanted me to be upfront and direct with her as she wanted to understand why I had always said that she alone was responsible for attracting the relationships she had had. As she cried, I explained to her the importance of taking responsibility for her life and letting go the need to blame others for her choices; that in doing this, she would be able to regain her inner power.

In time, Margaret realised that she had never really loved herself. In fact, she was frightened of being loved in case the person discovered an aspect of her they did not like. She had been criticised and found wanting for much of her childhood and had spent most of her adult life trying to portray herself as perfect. Self-honesty, self-love and self-forgiveness were vital if ever she was to find true happiness. I am pleased to say Margaret achieved this.

Most of the problems we have with other people are a reflection of the problems we have with ourselves. Any strong reaction we experience occurs because the other person's actions have collided with something yet unfinished or unacknowledged inside ourselves. When you are struggling with someone, you are really struggling with yourself. Every conflict is an excuse not to face some conflict within. Allow others to be, but work at communicating with them on an inner level by transforming your own feelings and thoughts.

When love is purely fiction!
We are all products of our family patterns, but we have to be aware in order to see them. I believe the most important ingredient in a family is love and that it begins with the art of loving oneself. Sadly, many families suffer from a lack of love and for those who profess to have it, it is often conditional love. I believe that, with love, anything and everything is possible. When you love yourself you can achieve whatever your dreams may be; when you add passion to the mix, miracles occur. When you are living your purpose, your dream, the Universe responds and grants you what you deserve.

Lack of family love has always saddened me - it still does. I've seen it far too often. Stories of abuse – physical, verbal, and emotional – have all too frequently unfolded within my four walls. It's never been my right to judge an abuser, but when I first started doing readings, I had to make a conscious effort to remain detached and refrain from moralising. What saddened me most was that these individuals did not know or believe they deserved any better; they just thought that was what happened in families. In many cases, because the patterns were so strong, the children would grow up to be abusers too, or marry and accept being abused. Some would turn to drugs or other forms of self-abuse.

One of the saddest cases I saw was Marcia, an attractive 21-year-old, who came to see me regarding her career direction. She was obsessed with making the right decision; nothing else interested her. She was driven by an inner need to be financially independent of everything and everyone. Her father was a self-made millionaire, who abused his wife and two daughters verbally and emotionally. Occasionally, he would resort to physical violence if he had been drinking; but as this only happened two or three times a year, his wife would accept it. Despite his wealth he had a fixation about money. His wife had to account for every cent spent on food, general household expenses, and even clothing.

Marcia had moved out when she was 16 and rarely visited her family. She phoned her mother two or three times a week but they hardly ever saw each other in person. Her younger sister lived with her boyfriend, who, according to Marcia, was as violent and abusive as their father; not knowing any better, her sister believed it was a normal relationship. Marcia felt her parents would remain married. Her father would stay because he had someone to abuse and control. Her mother was scared at the thought of living alone and having to support herself.

Marcia, on the other hand, had no interest in a serious relationship, let alone marriage and having children. She believed all males became abusers eventually. She found it difficult to trust and felt there was no such thing as love between two people. She believed it only existed in television soap operas and romantic novels.

Whatever I said was met with disbelief and denial. As I watched her walk away after the reading, I prayed she would find it somewhere within as the years unfolded for her. The thought that she could spend another 60 or 70 years in the loveless state she had lived in so far saddened me. Her passion for her career would give her some sense of purpose; I knew she would become extremely successful, simply because it was the only thing she focused on. As the universal law goes, 'What you focus on is what you will create'. Maybe that love would eventually flow within and attract a like-minded person and perhaps together they would come to experience true love and happiness.

Another sad story was Wendy's. She was in her 40s when she came to see me. She had married young to escape an abusive upbringing. Because she had not dealt with the abuse she had suffered as a child, she married someone who emotionally and mentally abused her. She had three daughters in quick succession, but her husband blamed her for not producing a son. He insisted it was the female who determined the sex of a child and used this as an excuse for having endless affairs. Wendy chose to remain in the marriage, convinced she was to blame for all the problems.

When she finally gave birth to a son she believed her worries were over, but unfortunately they were just beginning. Her husband had helped with the parenting of the daughters, but for some reason he left the son's upbringing to Wendy. He was very strict on the boy and often lost his temper and resorted to physical violence, in complete contrast to his attitude towards the girls.

In desperation Wendy visited a counsellor who managed to convince her that her husband was jealous of another male in the family. The counsellor explained how important it was for her to encourage and promote a better relationship between father and son. As time went on, the more she tried promoting this relationship, the further the gap grew. She worried constantly about her son's behaviour patterns and that he had very few friends. The school often referred to his anti-social behaviour and noted that his peers tended to shy away from him. She eventually gave up discussing her concerns with her husband, as this always resulted in the son getting a beating.

Shortly after the boy entered high school, she was called down to the headmaster's office and told that her son had confided to the school nurse he had been sexually abused. After considerable time, it was revealed his abuser was, in fact, his father and as the story unfolded, it became clear that he had introduced his son to child pornography. It was during the trial, that Wendy learnt her husband had suffered similar sexual abuse as a child. He was convicted of paedophilia and sentenced to prison.

It was only a matter of weeks after the court case that she arrived on my doorstep for the first time. I had never before felt so much anguish, guilt and sadness as I did when I sat opposite this woman. I always prided myself on being emotionally detached from my clients and their challenges – I needed to be in order to read them – but I honestly struggled to remain detached from Wendy and all her pain. Many around her judged and blamed her for the situation, convinced that she ought to have known what was going on. We, as human beings, are so quick to judge others without really knowing much about the circumstances. Often one can be living in a situation where everything appears normal on the surface, or one accepts it as normal, because one cannot bear to contemplate the alternative.

Sadly, I later heard Wendy had died of a brain tumour, without forgiving herself. The four children went into foster care, as the father was still in prison, and none of the relatives wanted to take care of, or claim responsibility for them. One wonders where they ended up – or how they ended up perhaps is more to the point.

What we resist will always persist
I cannot emphasise enough that by dwelling on the circumstances we fear the most, we create the conditions for those circumstances to occur.

Karen was 35 when she found her way to my door. She was stable, successful in her career and had a close-knit family; yet she had an enormous fear of remaining a spinster. Her two younger sisters had married in their early 20s and while she was very happy for them, she too wanted a husband. Karen came to see me every six months over a period of three years.

How many jokes have we all heard about people desperate to find partners and how many people have we privately judged for having this desire? I had males and females of all ages presenting with this issue foremost in their minds. If we are honest, we all search for a friend and partner, who will hopefully become our spouse. Why? I believe it is because we want to live in love, because deep within we know we are love.

Karen was an attractive woman and had no trouble meeting men. The problem was that her desperation and fear of never marrying was so strong that men sensed it and ran a mile. She put so much energy and emotion into this fear that she created exactly what she feared would happen. After many discussions, she finally recognised how she was obstructing herself; even so, it took another two men to walk out on her before she agreed to try my approach.

I advised her that in her next relationship, anytime she felt the familiar feeling of desperation and fear of not 'catching him', to acknowledge it and tell it to go away. I suggested that she focus on the positive aspects of the relationship – how well they communicated with each other, the love they felt for each other – and dispense with the fears. Three relationships later, Karen is now happily married with twins.

It is the fear we create in our minds that cause the problems, rather than anything outside ourselves. What we resist will always persist. By confronting our fears, we relinquish their hold over us.

Dying for love
Vivian was another sad case. She lived in one of the most prestigious areas of Christchurch; her husband had a successful business and money flowed freely. But the marriage was loveless. By time she came to see me she was in her early 50s. Her husband had had many affairs and blatantly flaunted his mistresses. She had caught several sexually transmitted diseases from him; but still she stayed.

Vivian spent a lot of energy convincing herself that, because her husband didn't physically abuse her, he was treating her okay. Her reason for staying had been to give her three children a stable family life.

By the time she had come to see me two of them were married and the third was living overseas; but she continued to stay so that this daughter could get married from the family home as the other two had done. She also believed she needed to remain married in order to show her grandchildren what constituted 'a stable family'.

Alas, the older the husband became, the younger the mistresses were. Then one of them decided she wanted to live with him and experience the gracious lifestyle. Ultimately, she convinced Vivian's husband that what they had together was true love; and he filed for divorce. Within 18 months of the divorce, Vivian had undergone three cancer operations and, sadly, had died in a hospice - full of bitterness towards her husband.

Over time, the three children witnessed how happy their father was with his new partner. Family gatherings took on a whole new meaning with all members refusing to play the victim game. Perhaps this was the gift Vivian had inadvertently given her family, but, unfortunately, it was at the expense of her own life.

Make me happy!
Through experience I have learnt that the way to change your circumstances or situation is to change the way you think and talk about yourself. What you believe is what you have learnt through your parents, schooling, society and your experiences. Your experiences shape your beliefs and

negative beliefs limit the truth of who you really are. When you choose to alter them, a miracle happens and what you perceive as your reality undergoes dramatic change too.

I encouraged my clients to re-evaluate their beliefs frequently and, if they have become an obstacle to your spiritual growth, to discard or modify them. Some would ask how they would know and my answer was "If the changes uplift you and enhance your life, then they are right for you at that moment". When you look at nature, you see that every living thing is constantly moving, growing and evolving. What does not, stagnates and eventually dies. This is another universal law, as illustrated by the following two stories.

Trudy was in her 30s and married with two daughters when she came to see me. Trudy believed, like her mother, that in order to be a good Christian wife, she had to serve others. Unfortunately, like her mother, she believed there were certain things in life she had a duty to do. She lived her life in bondage to these beliefs, and so she attracted a husband who was a carbon copy of her father, and who controlled her every move and thought. Her husband's rationale for this was that he loved her very much. She felt stifled, with no freedom to grow as an individual, nor was she free to express herself.

She asked me how she could change her husband. I explained there was no way she could change another person so her only option was to change herself. When she asked what changes she should make, I suggested she let go of the idea there were certain things she ought and should do for the sake of convention or out of a sense of duty and instead express herself as she wanted to be. I said that once she stopped serving others to the detriment of herself, the relationship with her husband would change; and that it was time to start loving herself. I didn't see her again, but then I didn't really expect to. I knew her beliefs were far stronger than her desire for change. I never found out whether she attempted to change her husband, but I guarantee the end result would have been disaster.

Denise was in her mid-40s when I first met her, though she looked 10 years older. She had spent most of her life putting herself down because she never thought herself good enough. When good things came along, and they were rare, she believed it was simply good luck; she felt she didn't deserve anything. Her husband had left her years before and she had brought up three sons on her own. She had believed it would be a struggle and, therefore, a struggle it was. Her boys' behaviour towards her mirrored how she felt about herself; they saw her as a doormat and someone to abuse when they felt like it. This upset her and she asked me where I believed she had gone wrong as a mother. She wanted to know what she could do to change their attitude towards her. I explained that no one can change others. You can only change yourself.

Her first step was to change her opinion of herself. I explained the concept of self-affirmation and how to fill her mind with positive thoughts about herself – that she did deserve respect and did deserve to experience good things happening for her. I shared with her a powerful principle – that of taking responsibility for her own thoughts, words and actions. In doing this she would be taking back her power.

Denise had a lot of underlying anger, railing at 'life' for what it had dished up to her. I knew if she could accept she had created all the circumstances and situations in her life that had led to this anger then she could change her life around. It took time but, eventually, Denise applied these principles and attended our workshops and her life changed for the better. The sons also changed after witnessing the change in their mother. What powerful scenarios we create to learn our lessons!

When love is found!

Clare came to me for business readings; I knew never to bring up personal issues, nor did I speak in too much detail about spirituality. I could always sense what a person would accept and his or her level of understanding. However, with Clare I constantly found myself throwing in something that challenged her to a deeper understanding. She saw the sessions as an opportunity to be forewarned about future happenings in her business. Our meetings continued thus, until a close friend of hers died of leukaemia.

She visited me often as she went through her grieving process and we talked at length about the meaning and purpose of life. She realised there was little love in her life; love had never been mentioned in her childhood. She said she had fallen into her first marriage and the various relationships since her divorce. At the time she had come to see me she had been going out with a chap for almost two years, though the relationship was more one of convenience than romance.

It was this realisation that set her on a path to know and love herself for who she really was. She attended our courses on self-development. The more she learnt about herself, the more she changed. Her partner, who was as unemotional and reserved as she had previously been, struggled with these changes; and when she expressed her love for him he took fright and called the relationship off. This is an example of the Law of Reflection in action.

It was not long, however, before she attracted someone who was more loving, like her new self. Six months later, Clare's ex-partner arrived, wanting to walk a similar path. He attended our courses and I watched with eager anticipation. Unfortunately, his real intention was to regain his relationship with Clare, and when that did not happen, he decided to leave New Zealand, convinced that it was our courses that had ruined their relationship. I believe his fear far outweighed his desire to discover inner love.

Many people, for a variety of reasons, will try and rescue their loved ones from this kind of philosophy in the belief they are helping them, when in truth they are hindering both them and themselves. I have done it myself with my own children. (Oh how I have changed!) Therefore, I cannot emphasise enough the importance of allowing others to make their own choices. Maybe they will make mistakes and perhaps experience failures, but all the while they will be creating opportunities for their soul to grow. Walk your own path and allow others to walk theirs. This is the greatest gift of love you can give.

6
Moving with Spirit

♥ *When the nightmare became the dream*

♥ *And it's all their fault!*

♥ *Look out! I'm climbing out of the hole*

♥ *Choosing to believe*

♥ *How dreams turn into reality*

♥ *When love was felt*

Moving with Spirit

I cannot over-emphasise the importance of discovering and living your destiny. When you do this, the Universe will always assist you. Be true to yourself and share the gifts and talents you bring into the world. Focus your energy on what you would like to see happen rather than on what is going on around you. There is a universal law that states 'Everything you think, say and do creates your tomorrow'. This includes your motive and your intent. When you yearn for something with all your heart and soul, you will make it happen.

When the nightmare became the dream

I remember Carol coming to see me regarding a business she and her husband Gary dreamed of creating together. Gary was a qualified tradesman and had worked in a variety of companies, in his search for fulfillment. When their two children had reached school age, Carol had taken a job in a friend's tearooms to help with the family finances. They had both become interested in New Age teachings and had decided to sell their home and put the proceeds into a New Age business selling books, tapes, tarot cards, crystals and so forth. I informed her that I could not see this idea working and, therefore, did not recommend it. But even as I was saying this, I could see her mind was made up.

As I watched her go, I prayed for enlightenment to strike her before disaster did. Three weeks later, she rang me in great excitement. On a friend's recommendation, she had gone to see another reader, who had been enthusiastic about their project and had predicted it would be a success. She then proceeded to tell me how the house had sold without even going on the market and that the real estate agent had found a vacant shop in their price range. They believed that as it had all fallen into place so easily, it was the right move for them. Alas, before the year was out, Carol and Gary were advised by their accountant to shut the doors and walk away. Walk away to what though? They had no home, no business and no jobs. Their outlook appeared rather bleak when they arrived on my doorstep one wintry Friday evening.

Over a cup of tea in front of a warm fire, we discussed what they could do to get out of their dilemma. They continued to reiterate their nightmarish tale over and over again, while I tried to direct their focus back to the present. What was done was done! I repeatedly asked Gary to put what had happened to one side and to think deeply about what else he might do that he was passionate about.

Finally, he admitted he had always wanted to grow plants to sell in the markets. At last it seemed we were getting somewhere. Of course, the next step was to make his dream a reality. Looking at it logically, he had little hope of making it happen. The couple had no money to invest in land, and had a recently failed business venture behind them. However, if one believes in the Universal Law of Abundance, anything and everything is possible. As we delved further into his dream we found some clarity – Gary had a strong feel for the holistic healing properties of herbs. He had read lots of books on herb-growing and the medicinal benefits they offered and had become quite knowledgeable.

While talking to him I could see his energy lift and the colours around him become clearer and crisper. Then he slipped back into defeatist mode. He could not see how any of this would be possible, especially as he didn't have anywhere to grow them. I explained how vital it was to keep his passion alive and that his 'guides' would be only too willing to assist him in realising his dream. His part was to ask them for assistance and believe in his goal. Belief acts as a magnet, attracting the people, events or circumstances necessary for you to achieve what it is you want to achieve. My clients were desperate and they had nothing to lose by giving it a go.

Eight weeks later they had made contact with a man in his mid-70s, who owned 40 acres of land on the outskirts of the city. His only son had been killed in a car accident in his late teens, and his wife had died three years before; now he waited impatiently to join them.

He agreed to lease 10 acres to the couple, who moved an old state house onto the land for the family to live in, and proceeded to grow garlic. Very soon the landowner became interested in their project and offered his assistance. He also became a surrogate grandfather to the teenage children, and his life regained a sense of purpose and meaning. This success story proves that with good intentions, hard work, passion, commitment and a little help from the Universe, your dreams can come true.

And it's all their fault!
For miracles to occur, it is necessary for individuals to be aware of the different signposts the Universe gives them. The majority of us have been conditioned to accept what life

dishes out, totally unaware that, if we search within, we will find the necessary abilities to create and live out our dreams and desires. This is our birthright as human beings. More often than not we make excuses to ourselves and others as to why things do not happen. We do this constantly in an attempt to justify our circumstances. We are experts at blaming everything and everyone – the economy, parents, life, society – for being the cause of why things are the way they are. This is what I call victim consciousness.

We ask our friends what they think we should do, but their advice is seldom adequate for our future growth. The only person who knows what to do is you; no one else can stand in your shoes. The answer lies inside us – feel it and bring it forth. For example, many people will come to someone like me for direction. Now, I could spout forth about where I see the client in, say, two years' time and, while that might be helpful, they have to feel the passion and possibility for themselves before any change can occur. There are certain things you can't change, but you can always choose your own direction.

I have always asked the client, "Where or how do you see yourself? What are the gifts you feel you have enhanced, or could enhance within you? What comes naturally to you? What do you see yourself aspiring to? What do you enjoy doing in your spare time? What feels familiar to you?" Many don't know and that's where my clairvoyant ability may assist. Often they will say, "Yeah, well that's something I have often thought about but I really don't know how to get there." We are all part of a gigantic jigsaw puzzle and each one of us is an important piece. While we are all connected, at the same time each one of us is unique. What we feel comfortable doing is probably something we have done in many lifetimes before this one. We come into this life with a purpose, but sadly, most of us do what is expected of us, rather than what we expect of ourselves.

Look out! I'm climbing out of the hole.
You have to know what it is you want out of life before you can start changing it. By becoming aware of how your own actions or attitudes stop you from attaining your goals, you can choose to change them if you truly want to. It is what we call in our courses 'your point of choice'. By letting go habitual patterns you change within; and as your inner world changes, so too does your outer world – sometimes dramatically. Grant yourself the freedom to choose the thoughts, words and actions that are the true expressions of your soul.

Make a promise to yourself that you will always come from your heart rather than react to circumstances around you. You will feel emotional calmness and glimpse intuitive insights from within a relaxed and healthy physical body. Strive to have choice and freedom in every aspect of your life. This fosters excellent opportunities for inner growth and creativity. Gradually you will notice that the things you once thought were important now appear trivial.

Justin was 18 when he first came to see me. He was an only child, as had been his mother. His parents had never married and for the first five years of Justin's life, his mother had fought a paternity suit. Because of this, Justin had known conflict and confrontation from an early age. Finally, his father had grudgingly accepted his role, but the resentment remained. Occasionally, Justin would receive a present for his birthday, but never at Christmas. For his 16th birthday he received a pair of shoes. When he brought up the issue of Christmas presents, his father replied "One shoe for your birthday and one shoe for Christmas. Count yourself lucky!"

He later described this statement as having caused him such distress that he fell into a pattern of alcohol and drug abuse, which culminated in his being admitted to hospital with an acute attack of the pneumonia he had suffered periodically throughout his life. After he was discharged he came see me. We talked about how often he had been made to feel he was a burden or a noose around his mother's neck. I helped him to realise that many of the things his mother had said to him were born out of the resentment she felt towards his father and had nothing at all to do with him.

The more he explored and discovered himself the more he changed, until finally his mother noticed a difference in his attitude toward her. If ever she tried to blame him for anything that went wrong in her life Justin would simply hand back the responsibility, refusing to shoulder the blame for her mistakes. Consequently, he realised that, by the same token, he alone was responsible for his drug and alcohol abuse, since it was he who chose to react in the way that he did in response to his father's attitude. He refused to listen to his mother blaming his father for everything and chose instead to follow his own path.

I lost touch with him until he was 20, when he called for another appointment. Old family patterns and beliefs run deep and can be subtle in their manifestation. For the past two years he had studied what his mother believed he should study rather than what interested him. He had started three different courses but had completed none of them, leaving him without any qualifications and an ever-mounting student loan debt. His purpose in coming to see me was to discuss a get-rich-quick scheme, which he hoped would solve his financial problems. It involved selling and talking to large groups of people. This was not something that came naturally or easily to him; but throughout his life his mother had told him that you worked to pay the bills and survive; enjoyment didn't come into the equation.

I asked him to recall what he had enjoyed doing best between the ages of seven and ten. Because his mother had been sad and angry most of the time, he said he had spent much of his time alone in his bedroom drawing and designing signs and labels for his toys. He smiled as he recalled the memory and I went on to ask him if he had ever considered a career in design. He replied "Oh that was for fun, a kind of a hobby and everyone knows that hobbies can never support you as a career." I informed him that this was merely an idea he had picked up from his mother; if he believed in himself and his abilities, he could indeed support himself doing something he liked.

However, there was still the issue of his student loan; by embarking on a design course he had be adding to it even more. After more thought, he decided to apply for a job as a waiter on a cruise ship for nine months. Mixing and living with large groups of strangers would help him overcome his inherent shyness, by facing his fear. Moreover, with the money he earned he would be able to pay back his student loan.

I am happy to say, nine months later, Justin began an arts and design course, which led him into fashion design and pattern-making. His mother watched his progress with pride and admiration; so much so that she decided to do the same course part-time. Now they are both successful pattern designers, working in partnership, and have successfully broken into the Australasian market. How? By breaking through their belief systems and family patterns, they created change within their outer worlds.

Kylie came from a dysfunctional family, where she had been regularly abused by her mother, both physically and emotionally. Her father had turned a blind eye because he didn't know how to deal with it. Though the school had suspected abuse, Kylie had always denied it. When her father had been asked if her mother had abused her, he had also denied it and had said his daughter was just clumsy.

Kylie had studied hard and been an A-grade student, but it appeared her academic achievements hadn't softened her parents' attitude; instead they had seemed to resent her for it. Just before her 20th birthday, she had married a man who also came from a dysfunctional background. Despite this, her husband's family had seemingly welcomed her with open arms; but it later transpired that this had been mostly relief, for there had been rumours over his sexual orientation.

Initially, all had gone well. Kylie felt she had finally found love, acceptance and a sense of belonging. But in reality she was deceiving herself. They lived just round the corner from the husband's parents, so as to be close to them. Kylie had an honours degree in journalism; however, her husband, who was constantly in and out of different jobs, felt threatened by it in some way and so she didn't use her skills. Instead she yielded to the whims and wishes of the family. What she wore, where she worked, how her hair was styled and cut, were all decided by her parents-in-law. Her father-in-law arranged a job for her as a part-time receptionist at a friend's car yard. He also chose the house the young couple bought and the cars they owned. Despite all of this, everything appeared to be going well until the husband's issues with his sexuality finally surfaced in the fourth year of the marriage. Her in-laws blamed her for not being a good wife and so, too, did her own parents. Accustomed as she was to being at fault, Kylie left, convinced she was responsible for the marriage failure.

It was at this stage that she ended up on my doorstep, looking for some understanding of her situation. She attended some of our workshops and in time found inner strength and self-confidence. Within six months of separating from her husband, she landed a job as a reporter on a small Christchurch newspaper. Before the year was up, she had moved to Auckland and was working on a magazine.

Two years later, she returned to Christchurch for the christening of a friend's baby, and visited me for another session. I was thrilled to see the change in her. By this time she had been offered a job in Sydney on a well-known women's magazine. Six months later, she rang me from Auckland to say she was off to Australia. She spoke of her parents' recent visit to Auckland, which had enabled her to see the growth in herself. No longer had she spent time and energy on seeking their approval or trying to please them; at last she was her own person. She referred to her past marriage as an opportunity for her soul to learn a major karmic lesson – never compromise or relinquish control over your life. I knew then that she would fly, for she had learnt a powerful lesson and would remember it forever.

This reminds me of another client, Amanda, who was in her mid-30s when she came to see me. Amanda was brought up in a small town in the South Island, where everyone knew everything about everyone else, or thought they did. On leaving school, she worked at the local supermarket while she waited to marry a local boy, just as all the other girls had done. There was little joy in life because there was very little hope and certainly no dreams to fulfil. She learnt to feel lucky that she had a job, for there was a lot of unemployment in the town and you took what you could get, whether you enjoyed it or not. Leaving the community was something only other people did. Life for the majority of young people was marrying early, settling down and having children.

On turning 20, she married the boy down the road and by the time she was 28, she had two daughters aged five and seven. Every Friday night, while her husband was with his workmates at the local pub, she would collect fish and chips for herself and the girls, then wait for two or three friends, whose husbands were also at the pub, to call around with their casks of wine. One evening, while waiting for her dinner order, she overheard a conversation between a staff member and a friend. They were discussing their latest relationships: which one would get married first and what plans or hopes they had for their future.

She told me it was like "listening, talking to my best friend ten years ago and I wanted to stand up and shout, 'No, don't do this to yourselves'." As she walked out of the shop she knew somewhere deep inside, that there had to be more to life and come hell or high water, she was going to find it.

Over the next few weeks she tried to tell her husband how she was feeling and attempted to explain her need to leave the community in search of a different life. Her husband refused to listen and the more he avoided her, the more frustrated she became. Finally, he told her to sort herself out and forget about leaving the area because he had no intention of shifting. Within six months she had come to the conclusion that, while she loved her husband, she was not in love with him, so she packed up their belongings and moved to Christchurch with her girls.

For a few months she struggled within herself to find the independence she so desperately craved. Different relationships came and went as she sat on an unemployment benefit, never thinking about finding a job. She was so accustomed to being financially dependant on others, that she transferred this dependence from her husband to being a beneficiary, and could not, or would not, see it any differently.

It was at this stage that she came to see me regarding the breakdown of her most recent relationship. On realising she was on a benefit, I questioned her about where she saw her life heading in terms of a career. Her reply was "Oh, success in careers and such-like are for others. I come from a small hick town where no one goes anywhere in life and I don't think I am any different. I left; that was big enough for the likes of me." The rest of the session was spent on her relationship scenarios, but when we said goodbye I knew it would not be long before she was back - to talk about a career.

Three months to the day, there she was again sitting opposite me. Her eldest daughter, Sasha, had always loved music and dancing and the school she attended was strong in performing arts. Sasha had dreams of becoming an actress and singer, and had taken the lead role in the school's end of year performance. Watching Sasha striving towards her dreams had stirred something within Amanda. If Sasha had the passion to follow a dream, why couldn't she? Amanda was now on the search to find hers.

We tossed a few ideas around and finally she realised her interests lay in motivating others. "Motivating others?" I queried. Yes, she exclaimed. Friends had always come to her for ideas on ways to create change in their lives. I guess the look on my face prompted her to add that she was good at giving advice to others, but not so great in following it herself. Amanda set to and contacted an organisation that trained people as life coaches, and turned her life around. Now she is self-employed, assisting others to achieve their potential.

Choosing to believe

In coming to someone like me, an individual can be forewarned of events and choices to come. One of my very early readings illustrates this point. Neil was in his mid-40s, married with three children and employed as a maintenance worker in a holiday complex at a small resort. Half an hour into the reading, he revealed to me that he did not really like his job and had only taken it because of the cheap accommodation that was part of the salary package. He and his wife would have preferred living in a larger town, with a warmer climate. Moreover, what he really wanted to do was to work outside on the land.

Recently an elderly aunt had died leaving him some money, and the couple were now thinking of moving to Marlborough, where he could find work in a vineyard or orchard and there would be more work opportunities for his wife. In my mind's eye, I pictured the family in Marlborough; but suddenly I picked up that his wife had a distant cousin living on the outskirts of Nelson, which he later confirmed. I advised him to contact the cousin, as he would know of any opening available. Neil's face was a picture as he exclaimed that they had learned of this relative only a few days before, and that he owned an orchard just out of Nelson. But suddenly anxiety set in – houses were so expensive up there, it would cost a lot to move – he trotted out all his fears.

Within minutes I knew that if Neil took some time off work and went to Nelson, contacted the cousin regarding work and asked him for the name of his favourite real estate agent, he would be led to a three-bedroom house. I described the layout of it in detail, explaining that a marriage break-up had forced the owners into selling. Moreover, the house was going cheaply because of some uncompleted building work.

Two months later, Neil arrived with his wife in tow. He had gone to Nelson, secured a job with the cousin and connected with the real estate agent. He had spent the afternoon looking at various homes but none of them matched my description. However, on returning to the real estate office, another salesperson happened to mention a house he had just listed that fitted the description; but that it needed a lot of work. The upshot was that Neil and his family fell in love with the home, bought it and, within a month, they had moved to Nelson. This, to me, is a true example of someone trusting that what they want and the need will be provided by the Universe.

A piece of advice I have given my clients is that every challenge and opportunity encountered is an invitation to step into the next level of consciousness. Every choice you make creates an experience – choice equals creation. The Universe, and those around you in spirit form, want you to achieve your destiny. The use of positive words and thoughts change the feelings you have inside; create feelings of empowerment and strength. Correspondingly, negative words are disempowering and any sense of purpose drains away.

There are some individuals who choose to lose control of events and circumstances by allowing their lives to be controlled by fate. Fate, I believe, is created by relinquishing your power to others. Take control of your choices and become responsible for your life. It is fear that stops people from doing this, so kick it out of your reality. When you experience a fear of stepping into the unknown, then it is time to call on your master within. When you confront your fears, they fade away. Don't waste time asking others; ask yourself, for only you will know what is right for you. We all have a path to walk, so take time to find your own path and stop looking at the paths others take. Read the signs from the Universe, for it will always have your best interest at heart and, if you listen, you will be guided to your true pathway.

I first met Erin when she was in her late 20s. She had been living in Wellington for five years working as an accountant. Her father's death from a heart attack was not unexpected as he had been suffering from heart problems for years. Within six months of his death, Erin's mother decided to leave Christchurch and move to Southland to be closer to her family. When Erin heard this, she did not hesitate to resign from her employment in order to help her mother shift. Everyone around her was against this decision but she did it anyway. I can still hear her saying to me "I just knew I had to do it. I felt it was right in every bone of my body. There was no way I would not help Mum move house."

This exercise took three months, but what she learnt about herself in those three months was breathtaking. Her whole energy level changed as she reviewed how she perceived herself to be and what she really wanted in life. Over this period she took a long hard look at herself, made some major changes within and then decided what she wanted to create in her life. Because she changed her inner self, her outer world altered accordingly. In the past she had felt forever grateful for what was available to her, not realising that she was capable of creating what she wanted. Three months later she had returned to Wellington and had secured the sort of job she had always wanted – share brokering.

In this new career she also found the man of her dreams. Eighteen months later, they married and life could not have been better for her. If only more individuals realised how magic happens when you follow your dreams, and listen to what your inner self is saying to you. Usually it is our fears that stand in the way of our happiness, but fears are just illusions created by our minds.

How dreams turn into reality
The power of creation is within all of us, yet so few individuals realize this. I met Kim when she came to see me because she was having difficulty getting pregnant. She came from a small rural area where her father was a farmer and she was the only daughter with three brothers. Her father was very controlling and her mother was submissive. For as long as she could remember, Kim had spent hours in her bedroom dreaming of a different life. Her father didn't believe in any home comforts or luxuries and the family home was spartan. Kim always believed she deserved better; and her mother's meek acceptance of the status quo irritated her. As a teenager she spent hours in libraries and news agencies browsing through magazines, imagining her life through the illustrations she saw. While her peers found relationships and talked of marriage, she immersed herself in her dreams.

At the age of 20, she moved to the city, where she worked in supermarkets packing shelves and doing any other part-time work she could find, while she studied fashion design at college. Erin saw her brothers, who worked on the family farm and did odd jobs locally, as being weak and dominated by their father; but there was little she could do for them. One of them, she said, was a manic depressive with suicidal tendencies; but she believed it was not her place to try and help him; he had to want to be helped. Instead, she continued to forge a career in the fashion industry and by the time she was 28 she had two fashion labels of her own.

Just before her 30th birthday, she took her boyfriend of nine months home for a week to meet her family. However, when she viewed him within the family setting, she realised he was very much like her father and she hastily ended the relationship. Her biggest fear had always been that she would end up marrying some one like her father, so much so that she had inadvertently attracted a similar character into her life. It is called the Universal Law of Attraction.

By the time she came to see me, Kim was happily married to someone who was the complete opposite; her only problem was her difficulty in getting pregnant. I recommended an acupuncturist who specialised in this area. I am pleased to say she is now the proud mother of two sons and a daughter.

When love was felt
I remember once, in the early days, watching a client get out of his car and walk up my driveway. Clive was a large, burly chap, dressed in shorts, with a packet of cigarettes tucked up under the sleeve of his tee-shirt. His arms were covered in tattoos and, as he approached my door, I remember thinking "My God! Why do I do this to myself? What a ridiculous situation to put myself in. I really need a dog for protection." Fear surged to the surface. At that stage I still had a lot to

learn about making hasty judgments - although it was obvious this man had a rough, tough past.

I braced myself as I opened the door only to see tattoos on his face of the type that are acquired in prison. He flashed me a warm smile, however, and I felt strangely touched by his openness. I didn't need to be clairvoyant to read in his eyes the pain and suffering he had endured over his 38 years. He explained that he had heard a tape-recording of a reading I had given to one of his friends and that he believed I could help in the healing process he so desperately wanted. I took his right palm, described his personality and character, based on the shape of his hand, fingers and thumb. I then explored the experiences in his early childhood by following the marks along his lifeline. These marks emphasised his difficult birth and the various forms of abuse – physical, emotional and sexual – he had been subjected to during his troubled childhood.

As I sit here writing this now, I can still recall his plea for me to help him with the pain of his memories. He admitted he had chosen to forget a lot of the things in his past. He could also see that his actions in inflicting abuse on others had been an expression of his own pain. He was well aware of how little love he had for himself or anyone else and that this had reflected in the violence and lawlessness of his actions to date.

He had done stints in borstal from the age of 14 and at 18 had graduated into the prison system. Female relationships had not been successful, though he'd managed to father six kids while he was still in his 20s. Given the number and length of his incarcerations, I was somewhat amazed by this. What had prompted him to search for healing was finding his eldest son as a fellow inmate. Interestingly enough, his son had been convicted for the same offence at 18 as he had himself. There are no coincidences in life. We are all co-creators of our individual lives.

As a result of meeting his son in prison, Clive was adamant that he wanted to change his life around. He hoped that by achieving this it would somehow influence his son. I explained my belief that we can only be responsible for our own lives; but we can certainly teach by example. He was very willing to learn and thus his healing began. We decided that he should come back to see me once a fortnight and I also gave him the contact details of a rebirth practitioner who might be able to help him deal with his past.

Clive's progress was gradual at first; he would often slip back into old patterns of blame and despair. But as we ventured into the spiritual aspects of his being and background, and as he became able to connect to his ancestral spirit within, the speed of change was remarkable. He spent much time at his tribal marae in discussion with the elders. I knew, at this point, there would be no turning back for him.

I felt privileged to share in his excitement about the reawakening of his soul. It was a beautiful experience and one I know I will never forget. I also knew that this was a turning point in my life. Eight months after seeing me, he went to England to sign up as a volunteer to help children in Kuwait. His past history caused a few obstacles for him, but eventually he reached Kuwait where he endeavoured to help traumatised children heal through song. He sent me postcards (with no return address) telling me of his progress.

Through meeting Clive I realised that the way to help any

client was to introduce them to their higher self, or the spirit within. Some may call it your guide; some may call it your guardian angel; whatever it is, or whoever they are, is immaterial. I believe the key to all healing resides within the inner realms of our individual selves. This was the wonderful gift Clive gave me. With this wisdom I set about creating a course entitled 'Connecting to your Higher Self.' This was the starting point of the courses I still run today. While they have changed, transformed and grown, as I myself have over the years, the essence is still the same.

I believe, when you travel down the pathway you have chosen this lifetime, then magic will often occur for you. You will witness and experience these miracles, as you learn all you have chosen to learn and you will automatically experience the abundance of everything you are and have ever been. Whenever you feel you are struggling and things are not working, stand back from the situation and ask the Universe to show you the next step forward. When the direction is clear to you, you will find events unfolding in front of you; synchronicity will occur. As I said to my clients, "Sure, I can give you a direction but it is important for you also to connect to the Universe." The Universe is there to assist and show you direction, so use it to your advantage.

7
Picking up the Dead

♥ *The truth is revealed*

♥ *Our love is forever*

♥ *Please hear me*

♥ *They see more than us*

♥ *I need your help!*

♥ *Because I love, I understand*

♥ *I have always loved you*

♥ *We believe it eventually*

♥ *Time to go*

♥ *This is not a game*

♥ *They never leave you*

Picking up the Dead

Early on it became clear to me that loved ones who passed over often took the opportunity to converse with those who remained. I believe their main purpose was to convey a message of love and connection, even though death of the human form had separated them. In using me as a channel, the client had an opportunity to consider that maybe there was more to life than the physical form which we can all see and accept. Because of my experience with my Auntie Maggie, my father and then my mother, I found relaying messages from a loved one very rewarding.

I believe that death is not the end of life, for the individual is very much alive. It's just that in our corporeal state we cannot see them. I also believe that, when you dream, you are actually with these individuals together as souls for that time span. There is always a purpose or a message to convey, yet many of us forget the message when we wake, though sometimes, when an individual is about to undergo trauma or hardship, they will remember having had a conversation with someone dear to them, who is now in spirit form. This perhaps explains the feelings of dread some people have before receiving sad news, like an accident or the death of someone they love. They have already been told about it in their dreams and some residual memory lingers on in their consciousness. Sometimes loved ones appear in your dreams to give you advice or direction for your next step forward.

The more aware you become, the more you will heed the message so lovingly given to you. Often you will be led to someone who can convey this message to you, though it may not be the reason why you feel you are visiting this medium.

The truth is revealed
One instance I remember fondly was when a Chinese woman in her early 40s came to see me regarding a broken relationship. She wished to know if I could see any possibility of reconciliation with this particular man. She held a senior position in a leading professional firm and within minutes of reading her, I became aware that any communication with the spirit world would be met with great scepticism. Fortune-telling was fine, but that was all she'd be prepared to accept. I proceeded with the reading, while at the same time I was aware of the presence of a soul who had been a strong male influence in her life.

The closer I came to finishing the reading, the more agitated and impatient this entity became. I allowed my own personality to take over, feeling the client would never understand if I mentioned the presence of this entity and, therefore, there was no point in conveying its message.

This is a mistake a reader can easily make if they allow their own personality to step in. If a soul wishes to converse, the personality of the reader is eventually put aside and the message is conveyed regardless; it literally falls out of the reader's mouth. The reason for this is that the soul who is present is wiser than the reader and can see the wider picture.

As I was removing my client's tape from the recorder, I heard myself ask her what her thoughts and beliefs were on where one goes after death. She was rather curt as she said she really had not given it much thought, nor was she that concerned. However, I said I felt compelled to tell her - in fact, I was being told to tell her - that since the beginning of the reading a man had been present in spirit form.

Her expression confirmed her scepticism but, nevertheless, I pressed on. I described this person's physical appearance as she had known him when they were together, and also relayed the mannerism that he so clearly portrayed to me. I think it was the mannerism that caught her interest. I then explained that he wanted to say he had been present at her mother's deathbed he had assisted her mother in moving into the spirit realm.

The look my client gave me was classic, especially when I let loose with the most important message he wanted me to convey: that he had experienced great delight in showing her mother the truth of what was really meant by life after death. I can still hear my client's laughter as she explained that her mother had been a very religious woman and had spent most of her married life trying unsuccessfully to convert this soul, who was her father, to her beliefs.

On his death, his wife had instructed an elder from her church to convert him posthumously so he could be buried in accordance with her religion. She believed she was saving his soul. This bit of information her father had shared with us was the catalyst for my client to begin her search for spiritual development. Through experience I have found that, when a personality is ready to receive messages from the spirit realm, their soul will lead them to the appropriate channels.

Our love is forever

I remember receiving a phone call from a woman who visited me regularly, asking if I would mind talking to a close friend whose grandson had died after a long fight with cancer. Daphne arrived on the allotted day, fearful and somewhat sceptical, as she had never met a clairvoyant before. According to her, I looked like a normal, average human being and very different from what she had expected. I could never help but smile when someone would say that to me. As the story unfolded, I learnt that the grandson had been diagnosed with cancer at three years old and had then undergone different forms of treatment before his death soon after his sixth birthday.

I proceeded to tune into the soul that had come with her. To do this, I blank my mind and allow the energy of the soul present in spirit form, to relay to me the message it wishes to communicate. When the human form is emotionally bound to a particular soul, I find that the messages come in fits and starts, depending on the client's degree of emotion. In this instance it felt more at a standstill, though the presence of her grandson's soul was very strong.

I encouraged her to talk about her feelings around the death of her grandson and the tears began to flow, releasing the emotional blocks which were preventing the communication between us. She explained that the rest of the family had been telling her it was time she picked herself up and got on with her life. She felt guilty, believing she was a burden to the rest of the family. This was especially true in regards to her grandson's parents, who were going through their own grief.

It was guilt that was blocking her from feeling any connection with the soul of her grandson. I endeavoured to explain the importance of acknowledging and accepting one's emotions without judging oneself; and within minutes the grandson was able to convey his message.

Daphne was sceptical at first, but when her grandson described the duvet cover she had brought him for his fifth birthday, any fear that I was hoodwinking her dissipated. The entity explained the depth of his and Daphne's soul connection, and the reason for having only six years together in this present lifetime. He talked in great depth about the lessons they had both chosen to learn through their relationship. He described the potential this had offered for the growth of their individual souls. He showed another lifetime where he had been Daphne's older brother and had died while at war. He also explained the reasons for these death experiences and the lessons therein for both their souls.

I felt privileged to play a part in this relationship between two souls and thanked Daphne for choosing me as the channel. I knew I had gained much wisdom from this encounter. Henceforth, Daphne began communicating with her grandson in spirit form. Over time she was able to assist and comfort others in similar situations.

Please hear me
Unfortunately, if someone is not ready to accept a death, the healing process is delayed. Charlotte was a 36-year-old mother of two children, whose husband had died after an asthmatic attack. Charlotte was so angry that he had died and left her that any comfort I tried to offer was thrown back at me with abuse. I saw him so clearly, standing beside her, but everything I said was met with scepticism and resentment. I

wanted to give up and let her go, but her husband kept on with the messages. I relayed her husband's christian names, his date of birth and also the date on which they had married, but still she was not convinced.

Finally, when I told her husband to leave, believe it or not Charlotte berated me for speaking to him in that manner. She said I should have more respect, especially as he was dead! I was stunned! Her healing began at that moment; I then understood why her husband had been so determined to get his messages across.

They see more than us

I remember another similar event. One morning, while doing some needlework in my lounge, half an hour before my next appointment, I suddenly felt a presence in the room. It was not intrusive, but, as I wanted time to myself before my client arrived, I asked it to leave. This it did, but within a few minutes I felt it back again, patiently waiting but with less intensity than before. I smiled and suggested the being might like to wait in my reading room.

My next client, Susan, duly arrived on time and I realised she had been to me before to discuss her then newly opened business. However, her reason for coming this time was to connect to her late husband, if possible. On entering my room, her first comment was "It feels warm in here, more homely than I remember." I smiled, well aware of her husband's presence, knowing she also felt it, if only on a subconscious level.

She wanted some advice from her husband so that she could assist with her daughter's choice of career. Her husband's message came through loud and clear - she had no place interfering with their daughter's choices. He explained that from where he was, he could see the wider picture; therefore, he knew their daughter needed the experience she would get through making her own choices. He went further, explaining that Susan's own lesson was to trust that their daughter would know when to change course along her career path. He also stressed that Susan was not responsible for everything in their daughter's life just because she was now the solo parent and nor was she as wise as her daughter's soul. Self-responsibility was their daughter's next major lesson. He could see the soul paths of both of them. He went on to say that it was time for her to let go any regrets, anger or guilt she felt towards him because he had never really left her, nor would he ever. I felt their conversation mirrored the depth of the relationship they had had when he was with her. Susan and her husband had clearly been together for many lifetimes.

Initially Susan was reluctant to listen and take heed of his advice, but when I repeated his next statement she became convinced. He said their daughter had shied away from responsibility all her life and that Susan's over-protectiveness was hindering rather than helping her. I had to laugh when she stood up at the end, waved her right arm out to her side and said, "It's almost as though he is standing right here beside me."

I need your help
No one should interfere in another soul's life, as is illustrated by the following story: Judy came to see me intent on making contact with her late husband. She wanted him to confirm that she had good reason to dislike her future son-in-law. In truth, however, the daughter had attracted a relationship that would enable her to learn the lesson relevant for her soul's

growth at that time. Judy's husband described this lesson and told her not to interfere. If she did, their daughter would only go on attracting similar relationships until the lesson was learnt.

All relationships have a purpose, and that is to give the souls involved an opportunity to grow and evolve by the lessons it provides. Once these lessons have been learnt, this type of relationship has served its purpose and the souls can move on. I had to smile at this soul's last piece of advice to his wife, which was to refrain from using emotional blackmail; not only would it do their daughter no good, but it would also harm her own growth because she and everyone else were governed by the Law of Karma; Judy had emotional blackmail down to a fine art, as had her mother. By heeding her husband's advice Judy could choose to let this pattern go if she wanted to. I don't know what the outcome was but I do know the Universe waits for the 'when' and not the 'if' in scenarios such as these.

Because I love, I understand
During my readings I have experienced the strong feelings of love in many soul connections. At the opposite end of the scale, conflict and strife have come through just as strongly. When the latter is the case those emotions are there for a purpose and if they are not dealt with, they will continue to return to the respective souls.

Pauline was a woman in her early 50s, who came to see me with only one question on her mind - Should she leave her husband? I began the reading by trying to unravel the tangled web of misery. Pauline and her husband had married in their mid-20s. They loved wealth and material things and worked hard to achieve them. They set themselves goals, which they achieved together and, after ten years of marriage, decided to start a family. Pauline gave up working in their import/export business, devoting all her time to being a good mother to their children.

The first born was a daughter, who reminded them of the husband's late mother; therefore, there was a strong bond between father and daughter. When their son arrived two years later, Pauline felt a stronger bond with him. When I looked at their birth dates, this was not surprising. By applying the eastern astrology theory, father and daughter were karmically connected, as were mother and son.

Pauline's husband worked long hours and he was often away from home on business, but she didn't mind because of the money. The children were educated at private schools and life was very grand until disaster hit the business and money became tight. The couple had a communication breakdown and there was a lot of blame and negativity. As the business fell further into the red, the husband drifted into a state of depression. Pauline felt lost in the turmoil and these feelings of resentment, helplessness and fear ricocheted around the teenage children. Pride kept the couple from seeking help and the whole family lost all sense of direction and purpose.

Pauline began taking anti-depressants and so, too, did her husband, who spent most days in bed wallowing in self-pity. The daughter, who had been an A-grade student, left school, worked in a supermarket and began drinking heavily. The son, while remaining at school, began experimenting with illegal drugs. Every one of them had lost their sense of self. I spent time explaining that they all needed to take responsibility for their own lives.

Pauline left the reading still confused about to whether to stay or go. Six months later she came for another reading; her son had just been suspended from school for selling drugs. It hardly needed me to point out that, while her son's behaviour was unacceptable, it was symptomatic of a wider crisis; the whole family was a ticking time-bomb waiting to go off.

It was this drama that prompted Pauline to get her act together and behave responsibly. She took control of what was left of the business, got herself off the anti-depressants and then started rebuilding the family. The daughter and son sat up and took notice and responded positively.

The daughter chose to do tertiary education and the son began to learn the ropes of the business and studied part time. Unfortunately, this turn-around came too late for Pauline's husband. He died of cancer shortly afterwards, still filled with shame and guilt over letting the family down. There was definitely a karmic connection between them all. We as personalities often think "Oh this is too hard to deal with; it's too much of a struggle; I must move on"; when in fact the karma may be to find the strength and courage to rise above adversity. In so doing, Pauline eventually hauled most of the family unit back on track again; and each of them learnt some powerful karmic lessons for the growth of their souls.

There was some interesting feedback on this family which I would like to share with you. About six months after her father died, the daughter came to see me. I had never met her before, yet when I saw her she seemed very familiar. Within the first five minutes of reading her, I saw her father very clearly, standing just behind her. She and her brother were still full of resentment towards him for dying and leaving them. They felt he had chosen to give up rather than supporting their mother's fight to save the family. In spite of this, however, she wanted me to confirm that what she was experiencing was indeed her father's presence around her. For example, she would frequently feel him in her bedroom at night and when she rode her horse. Often she would hear his voice in her head when she drove her car at night. (He had always worried about her driving at night on her own.)

By the end of the session she felt enriched, knowing her father had never really left her. Her acceptance enabled her to connect with him again on a soul level. Now she could call on him at any time and ask for guidance.

I have always loved you
Through my connections with souls who have passed over, I believe the way they are prior to their death defines their nature on the other side. I also believe they are then given further opportunities to change any negative beliefs and emotions they may have. I believe they can see a much wider personal picture and so can choose positive pathways, which will change their character. I am not implying that by dying everyone becomes a saint, but rather that they are given opportunities to make different choices. Because of this, it is possible that the souls I pick up may appear more loving or caring than their loved ones remember them as being.

I recall doing a reading for a woman named Rose, whose father had died many years before from alcohol-related diseases. For as long as she could remember her father had always been drunk; and she recalled her family life as being dysfunctional and wrought with pain and suffering. Her father was definitely sober when speaking to me and was desperate to explain to her the reason for his addiction. He spoke of love, compassion, caring, understanding and other qualities she didn't think he had known the existence of, let alone experienced. When I channeled to her that he wanted her to forgive him and heal herself, her anger bubbled over and she said I was talking a load of rubbish. (She wasn't quite that polite but I guess you get the picture.) She then related various incidents in her childhood that still devastated her. After her outburst, I sat there wondering why and how I had got it so terribly wrong.

Suddenly I heard various names from her father and where these people fitted into the family. Her disbelief and scepticism began to wane as he answered a string of questions she fired at me. Within days I had other family members visiting me, convinced I was drastically mistaken and intent on proving my messages wrong; but the scenarios he relayed convinced them and they began to see how much he had changed. He asked them all to forgive him, because he could see the damage they were doing to themselves by holding onto their hatred. He added that they had chosen this emotion in order to learn the art of forgiveness in this lifetime.

We believe it eventually
I feel compelled to share a story about a dear friend of mine, Mic, who struggled to accept me as a clairvoyant. He would refer to it as 'head-shrinking stuff' and dismissed any discussion with me on the subject of spirituality. He did not want to know about life after death, believing that once you were dead, that was that. As for conversing with spirits, well, that was not part of his reality.

Mic lived out of town and one evening he called to ask if he could stay with me for a couple of nights on his way to Australia. The day before he arrived, a friend of my late father's died of a heart attack in his sleep and I was aware that this friend, while in spirit, was struggling to accept his death. I called on my dad to help this individual pass over and I felt both of them around me when Mic arrived. Mic walked in through the front door and immediately asked me "Who has croaked around here?" (Mic was an Australian through and through). I began telling him that it was a friend of my dad's but, alas, he did not want to hear. He said that, if the spirit was determined to stay around, then he would find somewhere else to sleep.

Dad succeeded in moving his friend on and Mic, on his third beer, felt the departure of them both. The situation was never mentioned again. Sadly, Mic passed away five or six years later, but I was amused to hear that his children frequently felt him around them. One of his daughters said that, on one occasion, when she was in her bathroom, she saw Mic in the mirror looking back at her. His children, who are all in their 30s now, often come to stay with me, and sure enough, along comes Mic for the duration of their visit. I am so pleased that Mic now knows there is such a place as the spirit world and there is no such thing as death.

Time to go

During my time of clairvoyant readings, I became friends with some of the people who came for a session. I guess it was because we had similar interests. One of these newly acquired friends was also clairvoyant and intuitive herself. Often we would meet for lunch and share the experiences we had with the spiritual realms. She had a wicked sense of humour, which always appealed to me. I once recall the two of us walking back to her place after spending time at our local shopping mall. We were chatting away to each other, when my friend noticed an elderly gentleman walking towards us.

As we got closer, my friend asked me what I thought about the different souls that were hovering around him. She was confused as to why they were there; but when I looked, I saw nothing. The closer we got the more confused my friend became and, although I still saw nothing, I did feel somewhat uneasy as we moved towards his energy field. Just as we passed him, my friend exclaimed that his soul had just left his body and he was about to collapse. I turned towards her, horrified by what she had just said, when, out of the corner of my eye, I saw the gentleman fall over onto the footpath. People came running to help, but my friend said there was no point because his soul had already left. I was somewhat shocked by her outburst and suggested she should quieten down.

Eventually an ambulance arrived and we were all informed he had died instantly. Those who had heard my friend's outburst turned towards us. I hurriedly moved away, pulling her with me as she continued to talk about what she had seen. Fortunately the people around us were in shock and I managed to extricate myself without having to explain any further. This had to be one of my most awkward moments. My friend, on the other hand, saw it as a wonderful experience we had shared together.

This is not a game
At this point, I would like to advise you to think carefully before playing with the spirit world using Ouija boards and such like. I certainly do not recommend it. I have heard of many a scenario where participants in these games end up in all sorts of psychic bother, because they do not know what they are doing.

This reminds me of an incident that happened when my

daughter was flatting up north while attending university. Halfway through the year a new flatmate moved in. Often this individual would call on the spirit world just for fun. My daughter aired her concerns, but the female insisted she was in control of the situation and continued. Within a week the room in which the séances were conducted became infested with biting insects.

Having been brought up with my understanding and learning, it was not too long before my daughter felt the presence of different spirits within the flat. One night she woke with the feeling that a spirit or energy was in the bedroom with her. This encounter was not particularly pleasant and she became somewhat fearful. Instantly she called on the spirit of my father for help. Within moments she knew she was safe and that the unwanted entity had departed.

We often laugh now as we suspected Dad would have called the cavalry in for assistance! After a concerned call to me, I explained how she could protect herself and how to ask for assistance in moving the flatmate on. Two weeks later this woman had moved into another flat with others who also enjoyed playing games with spirits. The gift to my daughter from this experience was that she then became more aware of the presence of her grandparents around her.

They never leave you

I have often suggested to clients that they speak to their loved ones who have passed over. They are never too far away and are only too willing to assist or guide us. If you want to do this, I suggest that, just before you go to sleep at night, picture them in your mind. If this is too difficult, remember a fun or meaningful time you had with them and relive the feelings. Breathe these feelings deep in your heart, which

I believe is the home of your soul, and speak to them as if they were before you. To the sceptics, I recommend you ask for a sign to appear the next day, one that will confirm the conversation you experienced together before sleep. (I have heard some hilarious feedback on this.)

The point of the exercise is to realise that we are never alone, that we are always connected and none of us ever dies. You cannot die. Your physical body may be disposed of but the 'you' inside never ceases to be. You will always be somewhere close to members of your soul family or soul group, as it is often termed. That is where you belong, within a group of souls. All of us are where we are supposed to be, for we have earned that place according to our choices in consciousness. Never be afraid if you should feel loved ones around you. They do not come to frighten you but to let you know they are perfectly safe, and that death of the physical body means only that. I welcome the creaks, the flickering of lights and all the other signs that are sent to get my attention. I suggest you treasure the signs rather than dismissing them. I talk to my loved ones constantly and I keep them alive within the hearts of those still living by talking about them frequently.

My children, even though they never met their grandfather, feel they know him because of the stories I have shared with them. They were very young when Mum died and so they do not remember her, yet they have no hesitation in calling on either grandparent when they feel they need their assistance. There is much truth in the saying, "To live in hearts we leave behind, is not to die.' As I said earlier, you can never die, you just move to another dimension.

8
Spook Readers, Skeptics and UFOs

♥ *Alien invasion*

♥ *Saint or sinner!*

♥ *You see what?*

♥ *Strangers to themselves*

♥ *Blind faith*

♥ *My God, I'm a witch!*

♥ *The night I was suckered!*

♥ *Please listen carefully*

♥ *The genuine article*

Spook Readers, Skeptics and UFOs

A book like this would not be complete without the mention of UFOs and aliens. Clients have often asked me what my beliefs are in this area, especially those who have had encounters with these beings, or seen UFOs in the sky. I have never had this experience myself, but I do not dismiss their existence.

I once did a reading for an American woman, whose main reason for coming was to connect with her father, who had passed on a few years previously. He came through very strongly and I felt a healing process begin for her. Her father had left her mother and the family for another woman three years before his death and my client, who had bitterly blamed him for this, subsequently felt much guilt over their estrangement.

After a fairly emotional couple of hours, I was told by the other side that the healing, which the client desperately wanted, was now occurring. The door for her to experience life from other planets was now also open. My personality kicked in as I felt there was no way I could tell this woman she would encounter alien beings – not after what she had just been through in her reading with me.

But as always the spirit world could see the wider picture, and I heard myself saying that on her return to America, she would see a UFO as she sat beside a friend's swimming pool. The friend's name was given to me and, with much urging from the spirit world, I described her garden in detail. I went on to tell her that this encounter would change her life and that of her friend forever. My client looked at me in wonder and disbelief. Yes, her friend's garden was as I had described it; but no, she certainly could not, and would not, accept my story of UFOs and aliens.

About two years later, however, she wrote me a letter from America. Yes, she and her friend had experienced an encounter with a UFO while sitting beside the pool in the garden. As a result of this they had become heavily involved in a UFO group in California and life had changed in a most amazing manner. They now spent their days assisting others in understanding experiences and encounters with individuals from other planets; and the two of them were writing a book on the subject.

Alien invasion

About a year after my reading with this woman, two friends and I decided to spend a well-earned break together at Hanmer Springs, a quiet holiday and farming township north of Christchurch. One of these friends ran her own clairvoyant practice; the other was in the retail trade. She had belonged to a variety of spiritual groups, always searching for ways to develop her clairvoyant abilities. We stayed in another friend's holiday home and enjoyed a relaxing three days walking, talking and recharging ourselves.

On the third night, we went to bed just after 10 o'clock, exhausted by the long walks we had had that day. I was asleep the moment my head hit the pillow. I awoke with a start at eight in the morning, amazed at the time and how deeply I had slept. It was most unusual for me to sleep so soundly and, as I scrambled out of bed, I felt rather disorientated. I found my friends in the living room and over a cup of tea I was regaled with the goings-on during the night.

The friend who ran her own practice had experienced vivid dreams of being chased through the forest we had walked in the previous day; she remembered feeling terrified, but of what she did not know. My other friend recounted how she had heard an earth-shattering noise moments before her bedroom suddenly lit up with an eerie blue light. She swore she was physically unable to move but recalled being escorted by five unusual looking beings to a spaceship parked just outside her bedroom window. To this day, she does not remember what happened on the spaceship only the feeling of being returned to her room and made to go to sleep. She found it hard to believe that the two of us had heard nothing during this encounter. We did not ask the residents in the neighbouring houses if they had heard or seen anything and, as they did not approach us, we assumed they had heard nothing.

On returning to Christchurch, this woman's life changed dramatically. In an attempt to understand her experience, she put herself through a series of hypnosis and regression therapy sessions, hoping to discover what had actually happened to her during the time she had 'blanked out', but to no avail. She struggled with this for some time until she met others with similar experiences. Eventually, she joined a UFO group and began to assist others who had had similar experiences; in so doing she began to heal. She spent the following three years studying therapeutic massage, Reiki, aromatherapy and meditation and eventually found herself in spiritual healing groups. Furthermore, she believed she was guided in her healing by the beings that visited her that night at Hanmer; and felt 'more whole' than she had before. That was 15 years ago and I have never again been privy to that kind of experience.

Saint or sinner!

About a kilometre away from where I lived in Christchurch, was a Catholic Church. Every Tuesday and Thursday afternoon, a group of women would meet there to chat and organise different charity activities. The age of these women was anything from 65 upwards; some were married and some were widows. One of these women had been given a voucher for a session with me, as a birthday present from her daughter, who had already visited me. After coming to see me, this woman shared the experience with other members of the church group. The inevitable happened and many of them came to see me too. These sessions became a hot topic of conversation whenever they got together.

The priest eventually heard about me and, out of concern for his parishioners, and because of his own beliefs, he decided to make a time with me himself. I remember watching this man walk up my driveway and being perplexed by the energy field that surrounded him. I might add he was dressed in civvies and not in a priest's attire. I showed him into my room and explained the procedure to him. I asked him his age and he replied he was 39. I began explaining to him what it was I felt around him. I could see he wasn't in a relationship as there was no woman around him, nor could I see any children from any previous relationship. However, I did see other people's children, so I asked him if he was a teacher. On saying this, I also saw people from all walks of life and all age groups, leading me to wonder if he was a doctor. But no, I couldn't see any white uniforms around him.

All of a sudden, I saw the white collar and a church altar in front of me and then I realised he was a priest. I sat back in my chair and asked him why he had come to see me. Surely he had as many answers available to him as I had. He explained he was concerned for the women in the church group and openly confessed that he had wanted to check me out. I smiled, as I invited him into my lounge for some coffee and cake, as one does with a man of the cloth. He followed me into the kitchen, apologising in case he had offended me at all. I knew he was taking note of my children's bits and pieces that lay around the place, confirming I was an ordinary suburban mother. We sat in my lounge discussing our individual beliefs and came to the conclusion that it was a similar path we trod. Our intention to help others was what drove us both even though there were some philosophical differences of opinion. It was an interesting and profound experience the Universe gave to us both.

I remember a time when one of his female parishioners was in my room for a reading and two policemen walked up my driveway. I excused myself and greeted them on the doorstep. They had called to see if I could help them locate a missing person. I made a time for them later that day and went back into my room. The poor soul had wrapped one of the curtains around her and had her rosary beads out, busily praying. I calmed her down with a cup of tea and had to explain why the police had called before we could continue with our session. She was convinced they had come to take us away for breaking the law! A true example of how our beliefs can create fear in our daily lives.

You see what?

I had a string of people come to see me who did readings themselves. While I found it interesting meeting like-minded people, there were some individuals who claimed to be so highly spiritual and in touch with the other side that I often wondered why they came. The more highly evolved they believed they were, the less likely they seemed to attract clients and that was their major question. "Why can't I share my insights with clients? Why aren't I busy?" Some would answer their own question with "I am of such a high energy that I am being protected from the lower energies on the planet; and after all, only lower energies come to a psychic such as you." I always smiled and replied that I had never really seen it quite like that before.

I remember one woman who believed she had become spiritual and psychic three years before, after the death of her husband. She explained he was using her as a channel now that he was on the other side. Next minute she sat cross-legged on my floor with her eyes shut and her palms facing upward and proceeded to channel her husband's wisdom to me. Her visit was around the time of America invading Iran. Her husband's message was that President Bush needed to be destroyed and that he would be shot dead in a matter of months because of the upset his actions had caused in the higher realms. According to the husband, the gods had ordered this shooting and they had even chosen the person who would pull the trigger! Eventually, my client climbed back on her chair and asked me for my opinion of her husband's wisdom. I indicated that I found this fascinating.

Another psychic once advised me I had six pink panthers surrounding me and it was vital for my safety that I sent them on their way, as they were draining me of my psychic energy.

For a considerable fee, she could do it for me, as this was a regular pastime of hers. I declined her offer and thanked her very much for her slice of wisdom. Another psychic informed me that the purpose of his visit was to impress upon me the importance of acting on the advice he was about to give me. He attempted to convince me there were spaceships arriving from another planet in the near future. He said only those who lived by certain spiritual principles would be allowed aboard the ships. The majority of the world's population would not see the ships simply because they didn't live in that reality, owing to their low energy levels. When the last ship departed everything left on the planet would be destroyed. He had heard from various individuals that I assisted others to see aspects of the spiritual realms and, therefore, he was convinced I would be one of the 'chosen ones'. I replied how grateful I was to be informed of this opportunity to save myself.

Then there was the woman who spent the entire two hours telling me how spiritual she was. However, although spirit moved very strongly through her, for some reason it refused to help her in getting clients. She believed her estranged husband was constantly zapping her of her clairvoyant gifts and talents and that spirit was unaware of this, even though she told it frequently. She had come because she had heard I had a strong communication with spirit and, if she paid me – the amount being my choice – then I could tell spirit to stop believing the lies that her estranged husband was telling it. I tried to tell her it did not quite work that way but she left, insisting that, as her husband obviously had power over me, her visit was nothing but a waste of time. She concluded that I wasn't as strong as others thought. I merely nodded as she walked past me to the front door.

Strangers to themselves

There are also those individuals who are absolutely convinced that no psychic can read them. These individuals I find very interesting, as I love a challenge. They always have a big concrete wall around them and are constantly talking to the reader. Their energy fields feel scattered, which is how I feel when I attempt to read them. They 'will it' with their minds that they cannot and would not be read and, therefore, produce an energy around themselves that is so heavy and complex, the clairvoyant has to raise her energy levels much higher just to get through it.

In the beginning, whenever something like this happened, I would try my best to break through. Many readings later, however, I came to realise this was not necessary. If a client wasn't going to be open, then that was their choice. All I needed to do was wait and I would be shown a pathway. It was my ego that attempted to push forward, not my spirit. So I would sit and wait until I saw an opening. For a female client, it usually occurred through her child. For example, I would be shown a particular woman had a son and a daughter and I would also be shown their soul pathways at that moment. Once I revealed what I was being shown, the barriers would come down. If it was too personal, then I would see scenarios that I would not understand, but the client would.

Caroline was one client who was adamant she was too psychic to read. Once tuned in, I saw she had a son aged 19. I saw him around cars dressed in overalls and knew he was an apprentice mechanic. Caroline confirmed this was correct. I also heard the names of his friends, which I relayed back to her. Suddenly the barriers were down and I was able to read her with ease. Her husband's place of employment seemed to come through strongly and she said that, while he had worked there for eight years, lately he had become unhappy. I was then shown that he had felt overlooked and ignored during the latest round of company promotions and this had caused resentment in him.

I waited a minute and then described a male, whom I knew was an old school friend of Caroline's brother. I couldn't catch his name but I knew he could assist Caroline's husband by securing other employment for him. On receiving this information, Caroline's scepticism kicked in again and I felt the barriers going up. I tried to read the outcome but only picked up a void, so I turned my attention back to the son. I described an evening they had recently spent with their son and his girlfriend and as she remembered this experience, the barriers evaporated once more. Immediately, I was shown more of her husband's employment opportunities. Eventually, Caroline accepted that what I was saying could perhaps have some merit and she finally relaxed, making it easier for me to read her.

Suddenly I understood Caroline's attitude. She had spent most of her life being what others wanted and not what she truly wanted to be. She had worked as a secretary because her parents had insisted she do a secretarial course on leaving school, despite her desire to work with animals as a veterinary nurse. She had believed her parents when they said veterinary jobs were scarce and had allowed her passion to lie dormant inside. In truth, she had spent most of her life being too scared to reveal her true self to others, always trying to fit into the different boxes they wanted to put her in. In denying who she was, she found herself constantly erecting barriers when communicating with others. When I delved further into her energy field, I saw how she had become what others thought she should be, living by their rules and lacking any real thoughts of her own. Rarely if ever, did she voice her own desires.

Others who find they can't be read believe there must be something wrong with them, when it is simply that they are experts at hiding themselves from the world. These clients usually suffer from low self-esteem and are frightened that a clairvoyant will see aspects of them that they consider unacceptable. They fear they may be forced to look at something within them that they cannot deal with or will be judged for. These people need lessons in self-love and self-worth but they must come to understand that themselves. It is not for me to comment one way or the other; everyone has the right to make their own choices. Often they will allow themselves to be controlled by others and I don't want to add myself to this list of controllers. I can easily spot them as they have very little energy flowing around them and stagnant colours within their auric field. Eventually, they will hurt enough to change, but that can take many lifetimes and there are many lessons to learn along the way. It is never a case of *if* they will change, rather a matter of *when* they will change.

Blind faith

A word of advice to those who wish to take it; while a reader may be helpful in guiding one forward, it is important that individuals do not live their lives according to what a clairvoyant tells them. After all, clairvoyants can only give their impression of a situation and not everything they say will be correct. If clairvoyants insist that they are right, run! Individuals are making decisions and choices that can change their direction all the time. Therefore, what is said in one reading can drastically change in the next because of what has gone on in the interim. There are some things that will never change but many things that can.

Emma first came to see me when she was 17. She was about to leave New Zealand with her family because her father had taken a job in California. She came back to New Zealand for three months when she was 27 and looked me up for another reading. She was still single and had great career prospects. When I broached the subject of relationships and marriage she claimed she was waiting until she was 30 before thinking about that because I had told her when she was 17 she would be 32 before she got married. I quickly realised I had some explaining to do to Emma!

There was another woman, Marian, who came to see me about the health of her children. She had two sons and had been to two clairvoyants who told her she had one son and one daughter. She was beside herself with worry that she would lose one of her boys and asked if I could please tell her which one it would be so that she could make the most of his life while she could. It is so important to realise that a reader will never get it all right.

I also advise my clients that if they are uncomfortable with someone who is doing the reading or they are being told negative things, they should get up and walk out. No one has the right to predict negativity. In my experience, all information from the spirit world comes from a loving and caring place and those who reside there wish to help and uplift, not denigrate or predict doom. So choose who you go to with care.

I recall a friend living in Australia who once rang me to check up on a reading she had with a clairvoyant who had been recommended to her. For almost three years, my friend had been going through a healing process, letting go of the different aspects within her that no longer served her, and consequently she had grown immensely. Her business was flourishing and her personal life had taken off in the direction she had always dreamed of. In doing this she had moved away from various individuals, as interests and pastimes had changed along with her lifestyle.

At the beginning of the reading this clairvoyant remarked on my friend's high energy and they got into a conversation about the healing my friend had been going through, which had involved letting go of some of her previous relationships. After my friend had explained the effect these changes had had on her personal life, this clairvoyant went into great detail about how one particular friend had 'plunged a dagger into her shoulder' and that only she could remove it. Of course this came at a fairly high price, as spells and potions were involved. According to this clairvoyant, the person who had 'plunged' the dagger was of evil energy and, therefore, much work was required. Fortunately, my friend left without agreeing to any of this 'work' beginning. Her fears were put to rest when I asked her one simple question; "How come, if you are of such high energy, a person with such evil energy could possibly plunge daggers into you?"

There are plenty of so-called clairvoyants who will use these fear tactics to scrounge more money from their clients and believe me, in my 18 years in this line of work, I have heard many a story like this one.

In the early '90s, a group of practitioners in Christchurch set up a centre, where individuals could go for a variety of healing practices and spiritual learning. There were naturopaths, homeopaths, rebirthers, astrologists, to name but a few. One

Sunday, they held a psychic and spiritual fair and I was asked if I would mind doing some clairvoyant readings. So, as I had done before, I sat giving palm and clairvoyant readings for 10 minutes a sitting. Unbeknown to me, during the day the Sceptics Society had approached the organisers and, after some negotiations, it was agreed that the various readers and practitioners present would go on a live television show that evening.

On arriving at the television studios, I was picked to demonstrate what I had been doing at the fair. A client was picked at random from the audience, so I sat opposite him and spouted forth. What fun we had! The various members of the Sceptics Society had a field day with me, and I picked up much business in the weeks that followed. It was the best form of advertising I had ever had and what's more, it cost me nothing! I enjoy sceptics because they confirm to me the energy I represent. Their scepticism confirms there must be truth in my philosophy, for if there wasn't they would not be so afraid of it. So, I welcome sceptics with open arms and invite them to explore the spiritual realms as I have; then we can have some fun together.

My God, I'm a witch!
When I started doing readings in the late 1980s, there was not the same interest as there is now. Many saw it as light entertainment rather than a door to their inner selves. Spirituality was not as acceptable as it is these days either, and the majority of my clients were female. Males who did have some level of belief, or who were open to it, usually sent their wives or girlfriends along with a list of questions. But even then, there was a great degree of scepticism. The male clients usually heard about me from female contacts and almost never told their friends they had been to see me.

They usually came out of curiosity and I was often accused of having gone out with them. Hence the reason I was able to tell their female contacts so much about them. Needless to say, I always enjoyed doing readings for sceptics. I would endeavour to share with them some extraordinary bit of information they had always kept to themselves – like some deep, dark secret. The information I was given depended on how dark the secret was.

For example, Mark came to see me after listening to his girlfriend's taped session with me. He was curious to see how I would read him when I had never met him. He was convinced his girlfriend had told me different bits of information and was determined to give nothing away. He also spoke about my ability to read body language; and told me every five minutes about how sceptical he was and that there was no way I could fool or suck him in. He refused to answer any questions and kept repeating the mantra: "I don't know; you tell me seeing you think you are so good." When someone is as closed off as that it can be more difficult to pick up information because the energy does not flow between us so well. The way around this is to do what I refer to as 'going through the back door', to tune into information concerning their children or parents.

Mark didn't have any children so I asked spirit for a picture of him when he was a child. I saw him as a small boy in corduroy pants, aged about six or seven. I told him he was one of three children, the others being girls and that he was in the middle. I described the stripped jersey his mother had knitted him, with buttons on the left shoulder. The look in his eyes told me I had scored. The barriers came down even more when I asked him why he had cut the hair of his sister's doll and then stuffed the doll under the bed and blamed the family dog for the doll's injuries. He replied "My God, you are a witch!" All scepticism had vanished by the time he left my house.

Another male came to see me because his sister had gifted him a session as a birthday present. He told me constantly throughout the reading that it was a waste of time. He was adamant that I should refund his sister, as the information I had given him regarding his relationship was 'sheer and utter garbage.' Three months later he was back on my doorstep with a bunch of flowers and a bottle of wine, apologising for abusing me. He asked if I would mind telling him how the hell I knew so much about him and while some things hadn't happened, a lot had. By the time he left he had signed up for my next course on 'developing intuition' and eventually studied for a diploma in natural medicine.

The night I was suckered!
I remember in the beginning of my search for spirituality, I was invited to join a group of three woman and two males, all in various stages of spiritual development. Some believed they were more advanced than others. Whether they were or not I had no way of knowing, nor was I particularly interested, though I remember being in awe of these five enlightened beings as they spoke of different experiences and circumstances they had encountered, which were far beyond my experiences.

We would share the week's miracles in our individual lives and my life appeared very ordinary by comparison. They talked about conversations with their guides, feeling different energy around people and in different areas and places. It all seemed such mumbo jumbo, but oh, how I wished I had been blessed with this wisdom. After the talking, the lights would be turned off and the candles lit as we meditated with the help of background music. Try as I might nothing seemed to happen for me. Yet the others would come out of meditation with different messages for themselves as well as for members of the group. I heard nothing, felt nothing and saw nothing.

After three months, I decided to give it one more go before calling it quits, and it was that night I heard very clearly in my left ear, "It will happen, you must be patient." I got such a start, I disturbed the others but nothing could cloud my feelings of the immense aliveness I felt that night. I knew in every inch of my body that I was not alone, never had been and never would I ever be. An amazing feeling radiated throughout my body, ran through the blood in my veins and oozed out of every pore in my skin.

I could hardly wait for the next meeting to come. Oh the disappointment, when once again I heard nothing, felt nothing, and saw nothing. Back to square one or so it seemed. My heart ached. When it was my turn to speak I shared my disappointment with the group and as soon as the words left my lips, I heard very distinctly the words "It's now time to move on". "Move on? Yeah, sure," I said to the voice, "I'm trying but you haven't shown me anything." Little did I know!

Within minutes, one of the women began telling me that her guide had shown her a past life of mine and she was to pass it onto me. "Great! Now we are talking," I thought, but why had it come to her? Why wasn't I told? She proceeded to tell me of my life as a Jesuit priest; the different cloaks I wore and the work I did with underprivileged communities. She described my living quarters and the food I ate along with the other priests. I thanked her for this, yet could not figure out why I did not get the information directly. I pondered over this past life of mine during the next few days, but somehow it just did not feel right to me. I felt I could not relate to any part of this past life she had described. I threw it out to the Universe asking for confirmation. "Were my feelings correct or had I been a Jesuit Priest?"

At that stage of my life, my children were quite young and I had recorded on video one of their favorite programmes. I had been convinced that this programme started at 5pm, when in fact it began at 5.30pm. Imagine my surprise to see a half-hour programme on Jesuit priests. Everything I had been told at the meeting was contained in this half-hour of mistaken video footage. I then understood having heard the words, "It's time to move on". I had learnt a very valuable lesson, which was to always trust the voice within if I have any doubts about the relevance of other people's insights concerning my life. I don't believe that it was done with malice or ill intent. I was certain she had seen the same programme and as time soon revealed, her imagination tended to cloud her intuition. This is usually a case of the ego stepping in front of the soul; it's a common practice with most egos.

I remember in readings, that if ever my ego stepped in front of my soul, I would see the image of a high brick wall. I always knew on seeing this brick wall that it was my higher self telling me to shut up and go back to the path. I would then apologise to the client and say that my imagination had taken over my intuition. As soon as I would utter these words the brick wall would disappear and I would see another picture. I would then know that I was back on track again and could continue with the reading. It is very important for those being read to ask within if this is their inner truth. Honesty from both parties is required at all times.

Please listen carefully!

For those of you who wish to become clairvoyant readers, may I offer some advice based on my experience. People only hear what is real to them. Therefore, while it is vital to encourage a client forward, listen carefully to what they are being shown or told through you and make sure it is at a level they will be able to understand. There are some readers who come out with information that is well above the comprehension level of the client and then wonder why the client doesn't 'see it' or 'get it'. My advice is to be guided from above and, if you find your information is falling on deaf ears or going over the client's head, check to see it is not your ego talking. I guarantee it is. You cannot, as a reader, expect your client to understand what they have yet to experience. We all learn through experience and these experiences determine our level of growth and understanding.

Also, have the grace to allow your client to choose his or her own truth and values. Allow them the privilege of experiencing and learning in their own way and in their own time. When they feel it, they will know it. I truly believe it is important to allow everyone to be, and to accept them for who they are. As a spiritual sage once said to me "You cannot drag someone through a dozen lifetimes of understanding and experiences with expectations that they will comprehend everything you are saying." It's like giving an accountant a surgeon's scalpel and expecting him to operate, or expecting a hairdresser to build you a home just because he or she has some builder's tools.

Your reality is not always someone else's reality; this is an important lesson for any medium or clairvoyant to note. It is my personal belief that insights or readings should only be given with the permission of the one being read. I have often been asked by friends and acquaintances what I can read around a certain person. I never read another if I have not been given the okay to do so. Some people become fearful of me when they hear I have clairvoyant abilities. I sense it is because they feel vulnerable and that I may pick up something about them that they do not want disclosed. This would be an intrusion into someone's privacy and I very strongly believe that people's privacy is to be respected. I have met various readers socially, who start spouting forth about what their spirit guide, angel or whoever is telling them and insist that they pass on this so-called message. Bollocks is my answer to that – especially when the comment is laced with criticism. That is just ego talking. It has nothing to do with the spirit realms.

The genuine article

How do you recognise whether a clairvoyant or spiritual teacher is genuine or not? Ask yourself this: "Are they are coming from the heart and encouraging you to explore and discover more about yourself?" A genuine spiritual teacher will assist you to find, and listen to, your master within. The more you do this, the stronger you will become. Then you will witness the magic and miracles available to us all.

A genuine clairvoyant or spiritual teacher has no need to take anything from you. If you go to someone and they insist they know what is best for you, turn and walk away. If they predict negativity, walk away. If they insist on ridiculing your choices, walk away. Their intention is to strip you of your power, making you reliant on them. The genuine ones will never tell you what to do. Instead they will assist you in examining the illusions you hold about yourself and in so doing you will come to know who you truly are.

You have the power within to overcome all difficulties. Just remember that not only are you a human being, you are also part of the divine. So, I suggest to all my clients, surrender yourself to the divine power and you will feel the connection within. Then you will want to explore your soul qualities because of the uplifting feeling they give you. I will often challenge a client to pick a soul quality for a day; for example, kindness. Spend a day expressing kindness to everyone you encounter. Compliment strangers on their clothing, their hairstyle, anything you wish, and note the difference in the energy exchange between the two of you.

9

As above ~ So below

♥ *The two worlds we live in*

♥ *Stand aside, I'm talking*

♥ *Whisperings in the ear*

♥ *I'm in charge*

♥ *Come and have some fun*

As above ~ So below

Throughout this book I have endeavoured to share and explain the fundamental universal laws that I follow. As a clairvoyant I have shared with my clients how they can also benefit by understanding and then introducing these laws into their individual lives. I have shared their stories with you because they show the changes that have occurred for these individuals. If you can grasp the teachings yourself and use them in your own life, then I promise you, your life will change dramatically.

I feel privileged that my time as a clairvoyant has given me an understanding of the deeper mysteries of the Universe. This understanding has guided me towards making the decisions I have made in my journey within this lifetime. Life is not just about growing up in a family, or getting married and having children. Life is far greater than that. When you understand the mysteries of life and the laws that govern our Universe, you can create huge opportunities for yourself. These opportunities are available to us all but, if we do not understand the workings of the Universe, we miss finding the deepest parts of ourselves.

The two worlds we live in

I truly believe everyone is intuitive but some have developed their intuition more than others. I believe this development occurs over many lifetimes. Without my experiences with the spiritual realms, I feel I would never have come to know that we all live in two worlds. One is the physical world, where our personalities are dominant. It is a world of judgements and opinions and is very limiting. The other is the spirit world, which is filled with energy and love, and where everything is possible. Our soul resides in the latter. When we are in this spirit world we come from love. It is where we understand that everything is perfect the way it is. It is where we realise that everything and everyone is connected. We all live in this world even if we are unaware of being there, and in it we are able to create anything we desire.

It is my understanding that when I do a reading, I place myself in this world and can then read the messages within the energy field using what I refer to as my mind's eye. I can determine the feelings from the energy around any situation or person. This simply means I can see the inner world of the clients, which they are not necessarily conscious of, and I can share it with them. I have become aware I was able to tune into the spirit world in three ways. My strongest sense is clairvoyance. Through my mind's eye I am able to see an image of a person and I can then describe this image to the individual in front of me. For example, I would silently ask for an image of their home. Within moments I would perhaps see a wooden two-storied character home with a garden full of roses. If I were to tell you to think of your home right now, you too would see it in your mind's eye even though you are not physically there.

A client might ask me about a person they had just met. By

asking the spirit world, I would see that individual's physical form in my mind's eye. I would know whether that person was short or tall, the colour of their hair and any identifying marks or physical conditions they might have, for instance a birthmark or maybe a limp. After describing these images, I use what I call a 'feeling state' which is the clairsentience aspect of my gift. I would physically feel the atmosphere or energy field within the home; whether it was a happy or sad family life there; whether there was a lot of activity. I may even know who tended the roses in the garden. For instance, presuming that I was seeing a male, I would feel what was happening physically for him, whether he was well or ill; I would feel this in my own physical body. If he suffered from indigestion, I would experience this discomfort. If this person had an anger problem, I would feel the anger rising in my own body.

The third method of sensing is by hearing word messages. These could be names or messages for individuals, which were being conveyed to me by those connected to them in the spiritual world. This is clairaudience, which I have explained in more depth in the chapter 'Don't Shoot the Messenger'. I would always forget what I had said soon after a reading. Sometimes clients would ring back asking me questions regarding their reading. I confess I could never remember what I had said, so I would then have to tune into them again to answer their question. In the beginning I thought I was suffering some memory loss until I understood that the information I received was not mine to store. Nor did I want it. I was merely a messenger passing on information from the spirit world.

Most of the time I had no idea what the feelings, messages or pictures meant, but once I had described them, the clients would understand what I was saying. Then they were free to act or not according to the circumstances. If ever I found myself judging or expressing an opinion, then I would know that I had stepped back into my personality and I was in the physical world. As a reader, I was purely the conveyor of messages from the spirit world and had no right to interpret, with my personality, what I was given. I explained this in chapter two, 'Don't shoot the Messenger' with Simon and the two sisters whose parents had died in the Mt Erebus disaster. I believe everyone can visit their spirit world with guidance from their higher self, which is why I put together the course 'Conversations with your Higher Self.'

I believe the purpose of my intuitive gift is to assist others to see the possibilities and potentials which are available to us all through the spirit world. As we are spirit, we are part of the spirit world, which is the inner world within each individual. This world is not frightening; it is only our thoughts that make it seem so. Nor is it ever negative. Instead, it is uplifting, encouraging and supportive, as it assists us to learn our chosen spiritual lessons. The intention and motives behind all the messages I receive are positive.

I believe my intuition can assist others to see a situation from a different angle or viewpoint. This insight can offer a change in direction or attitude, which assists individuals to overcome their fears and thus move forward. I cannot say it often enough – fears are just an illusion created in one's mind or one's thoughts, based on things that have happened in the past.

Stand aside, I'm talking!
The Universe is in constant dialogue with us all. There are signs all around us. While sometimes we may feel we are

completely alone, I have no doubt that the Universe is our constant companion. Why? Because if I ask and wait to receive, the Universe will always confirm its presence by sending signs to assist me with the choices and decisions I make.

I recall staying at a friend's place in Auckland and sharing with her how we as human beings do not necessarily see the wider picture in every situation. At times, we can be quite adamant that we know or see it all, but often things are hidden from us for a reason. We were travelling in her car when I decided to ask the Universe for proof of this statement. As we pulled up at an intersection, we stopped behind a large four-wheel drive vehicle. Traffic was very busy as we waited for this vehicle to proceed around the roundabout. We waited patiently, still deep in our discussion.

Eventually there came a gap in the traffic, enough for the four-wheel drive to move but it remained stationary. Cars behind us started tooting, but still it didn't move. Suddenly, from in front of the vehicle, I noticed two men pushing a small red mini towards the kerb. Those who had tooted did not know there had been a breakdown. The Universe had delivered us a situation which reflected exactly what we had been discussing. We come together in circumstances and events so that we can all learn our respective lessons.

With the Universe as your constant friend you are always safe. Listen and take heed of your inner feelings. I can recall a time while holidaying in Australia when we travelled by car from Brisbane to Sydney. We had read in a leaflet about a lookout point up in the hills, just past Byron Bay, where you could see along the coastline. Not knowing the area at all, we decided to use our intuition to find the road to this lookout.

We were driving up a steep hill when suddenly I heard, very clearly, "Lookout on the right". As we slowed down to make the right-hand turn, a car sped from this very road, through the stop sign, missing us by inches. If we had not slowed down to make the turn, we would have collided. The words I had heard ("lookout on the right") had really meant look out for the car that is coming on your right. Needless to say, we did eventually find the lookout, but thankfully I heeded the message I had heard.

Universal signposts are there to direct you to where you are meant to be. For example, when I sold the family home, I spent many an hour looking at other homes to purchase. I had seen this house in my mind, courtesy of the Universe, and I knew without a doubt which area of Christchurch I would buy into. I spoke to a couple of real estate friends and told them what I wanted. I stipulated both the area I wanted to live in and my budget. Both told me I was wasting my time even thinking about it. However, I refused to accept this advice, choosing instead to believe the messages I had received from the Universe. I spent hours driving around the streets in my chosen part of the city, feeling the energy and wondering which house it would be. I went to every open day, patiently waiting for the house to come on the market.

It took 17 days of searching when bingo, there it was. The owners had purchased another house and needed to sell. I saw it, signed the agreement, paid the money and moved in. Then I invited my two real estate friends around to see it. I was so proud. This was the Law of Abundance in action.

I decided my change in residence also called for a change of career. During my readings I often saw the houses my clients lived in, so I thought I could take advantage of this ability. I reckoned that if I was in real estate I would be able to see the clients and know intuitively where to find their next home. It all seemed so easy. I spoke to one of my friends whose husband owned a real estate franchise. He recommended I sit in during some open homes, to see how it felt.

I was so excited, but right from the beginning it was a disaster. It took three open homes for me to realise that real estate was not the career for me. I had justified my decision in the belief that I would be assisting would-be buyers and sellers, while the reality was that I was attempting to use my abilities for my own gain; and my physical body retaliated violently with headaches, fever and vomiting.

Deep inside I knew my real mission was to assist individuals to connect with and understand the spiritual realms. So back to readings I went. I reinstated the Connecting to your Higher Self courses and bookings poured in. I changed the format of the courses and over time my soul grew and evolved along with those of my clients. When things do not go the way you want them to, it does not mean the Universe is against you. The purpose of life is to realise your spiritual nature, your soul's path and then your life will unfold as it is meant to. If ever you are uncertain of your true path, ask the Universe for guidance and a situation will present itself, either confirming you are on the right track or showing you another way.

I recall a story I heard from an enlightened friend, who was responsible for a number of staff in a large company. His instinct told him that a certain employee was stealing from the company, although he could find no proof of this. He discussed his concerns with two of his employers who both felt he was wrong; they had found this particular person loyal and devoted to the company. My friend was not convinced, however, and decided to spend a morning working alongside this man.

Later that afternoon he was travelling in a car with his employers, still thinking about this man. All of a sudden he began yelling to his fellow passengers to tighten their seatbelts as he felt they were going to have an accident. His bosses laughed and joked about his concerns, saying there was hardly any traffic around and that they were all perfectly safe. My friend tightened his belt and continued yelling at them to do the same. Within seconds, a car that had burst a tyre veered over into their lane and smashed into them. The impact caused their car to flip sideways and crash into the barriers of the motorway. My friend was unscathed but his companions were admitted to hospital with whiplash and other injuries. My friend took this as a sign and focused on the man he suspected of theft. Ten days later his suspicions were confirmed. He knew the accident was a sign from the Universe to believe what his gut feelings were telling him.

How many times do we find ourselves changing our plans for no logical reason, yet in hindsight we can see the purpose for these changes? A few years back, I was staying with a friend in Auckland for a weekend and booked to fly home to Christchurch around 10am on the Monday. I awoke on Sunday morning with a nagging feeling that I should change my flight to the late afternoon, so I rang the airline to cancel and rebook, without any idea why. On the flight home I had a conversation with the flight attendant, who informed me that the morning flight I had originally booked had been cancelled. The passengers had been rebooked on the next flight, which went via Wellington. However, because of windy conditions the flight had been diverted to Palmerston North and the passengers had been bussed to Wellington. There, they had been grounded by fog and the flight was due to arrive in Christchurch only a few minutes before my own flight. I silently thanked the inner voice which had told me to change my arrangements.

As I write about listening to the Universe, I am reminded of another situation. I often lease out my Akaroa holiday home over the holiday period. Two days before the first tenants were due to arrive, we went over to tidy the garden and attend to any odd jobs that needed doing. We discovered the old oven had well and truly died and had 36 hours or so to find another one. It sounds simple enough, but it had to fit into a small space. We drove back to Christchurch only to find that the newer slim-line models were just a little too wide, and we had no time to reposition the cupboards on either side. So the hunt was on for a second-hand stove. A simple errand was turning into a nightmare; we visited four different second-hand dealers without finding anything.

On returning to the car, I decided to tune in and ask for help. I was 'shown' a place in Lincoln Road. We drove out there, dashed into the shop only to find they didn't stock white-ware. The owner, on seeing my face, asked if he could help and I told him the sorry saga. He said he had an old one in his backyard and we could have it for nothing because his wife was constantly nagging him to get rid of it. I could have kissed him! We cleaned it up and it's been working ever since. We offered the dealer and his family the holiday house for a weekend as a thank you. Saved by my intuition once again!

Whisperings in the ear

I firmly believe that the Universe will adapt signs or messages to suit the inquirer, although it is up to each individual to ask for what they want. My most frequent requests are: "Show me the direction I am supposed to be moving in." or "Show me my next steps forward." The more you ask and receive the clearer the two-way communication becomes. If you are uncertain about the answer ask for further confirmation and learn to trust your intuition.

When I act on my intuition, I always feel more empowered and alive, but when I ignore it I feel blocked and drained and find things become more difficult to achieve. One of my intuitive friends would ask a question and then wait for a tingling feeling. If she felt it on her left, she knew it was her intuition; if she felt it on her right, she believed it was her logical mind wanting something to be so. Every one is different, so it's important to find out how your intuition speaks to you.

To hear the messages clearly you must practise what I call 'emptying your mind'. The way I sharpened this ability was through meditation. I have been asked many times about the importance or relevance of meditation. Personally I feel that meditation, or contemplation if you like, quietens the mind so the soul can be heard. Before I began this journey, my mind was very busy analysing everything that happened in my daily activities. I was forever searching for why situations and circumstances happened the way they did. I spent hours thinking about the people who had crossed my path and gave my emotions free reign. By meditating I learnt to slow my mind and gradually my emotions started to fade. I learnt not to put energy into the things I couldn't change. Instead I chose the path of acceptance; I would say to myself "It is just the way it is." In doing this I granted myself an opportunity to heal something inside me with love.

To meditate, slow the mind until it becomes like a blank screen, and think about nothing. In this state you can shut off from the outside or physical world, and connect with your soul. When you do this regularly you will stop looking outside of yourself for answers. Your soul knows what is right for you. Everyone has an individual truth. By meditating, you can unlock the door to that truth within you, and this will help you take responsibility for your life.

One of the activities we used to suggest to people on our courses was to select a soul quality for a day. Invite this quality into your world and then listen to your inner voice. You will then become aware, by the secrets it shares with you from the spirit world, of the areas in your life that require love. I guarantee you will learn a lot about yourself in doing this exercise. I remember selecting the quality of non-judgment for a day. That is, I was not to judge anyone or anything, even myself.

Before getting up that morning I asked the Universe to give me opportunities to practise this. I must confess that being judgemental was a bad failing of mine. I had arranged to do some errands around town – delivering school uniforms for dry-cleaning, paying bills, shopping for the family etc. Before leaving the house that morning I had received three phone calls from friends who spent most of the conversation criticising others. I didn't join in as I usually would have done. I realised that they were not aware of their criticisms, nor did they notice I wasn't adding to their stories. I found this quite fascinating.

As I started off on my errands, I made a conscious effort and watched my reactions as I was cut off by another driver at the first set of traffic lights. Then, I found myself behind a very slow driver who appeared to be lost. I never said a word but watched my thoughts carefully. Finally I drove into the car park of my local shopping mall, where I noticed an elderly man reversing out of a park close to the entrance. I put my indicator on and waited, giving him plenty of room to reverse out. He went backwards and forwards three times before finally driving off. I was so pleased with myself for not passing judgement on his driving skills. I put my car into gear but before even moving, a BMW roared past me straight into 'my parking space'.

I couldn't believe it! I sat with my mouth wide open and what's more, the driver appeared totally oblivious to my presence. I was being tested to the limit. I began to notice a number of negative emotional patterns I had cultivated over my lifetime. Through this realisation I learnt so much about myself. Consequently, when we put the material for 'Course One' together, we made this the first week's exercise.

A day of patience has its merit especially if you tend to be an impatient individual. I am often asked how to be more patient. The answer is by being patient. There is no other way to learn a soul quality than by becoming it. I now believe that the less I judge others and myself, the more love I feel and this assists me to focus on the positive aspects of myself and other people.

Clients often ask why, when they visualise and repeat affirmations, they don't always get what they want. There is always a valid reason for this, even though at times it may not be clear. Everything happens when it is supposed to happen. The Universe always delivers what it is appropriate for us to receive. My advice is to let events naturally reveal themselves. According to universal laws everything will be revealed in the perfect way and with the perfect timing.

While I believe we create certain events and situations for the lessons our soul needs to learn, there are times when we can change the next event by the choices we make in the present moment. I frequently get asked "Have I made a mistake and missed an opportunity because of my past choices?" I liken it to driving down a motorway with the desire to reach a destination. Somehow, you find yourself in the wrong lane and have to turn off into a cul-de-sac, and then turn round to get back onto the motorway. Was that failure or a mistake? No! Look at what you have learnt or how you have grown by going down that cul-de-sac. Nothing is ever wasted.

I'm in charge

One of the spiritual principles that had a major effect on me was learning to take responsibility for all aspects of my life. Theoretically this means being responsible for every thought, feeling and action I choose. When I first heard this, I thought "Oh my God. That's impossible." Eventually I realised that it was my choice how I felt or thought about, or reacted to, whatever was happening around me. I believed I couldn't change events but I could change how I felt about them. As time went by, I stopped reacting with my mind and emotions; I observed how I felt. In not reacting I found my power and strength within. When I realised that my decisions were mine alone, I knew that no one and nothing had power or control over me. I then understood that everything that happened in my life was created by me; and I realised that anything I didn't like I could change, just by changing my thoughts.

I believe it is vitally important for your health and happiness to look within to discover your individual destiny and then go and do it. It is your responsibility to find and express your passion. It is your responsibility to realise what it is you have to do to fire this passion inside of you. To experience happiness and love you have to be in the process of accomplishing your dream and destiny. When you do this, the Universe responds by helping you achieve your dreams; as does your soul group in the other realms. That is what they are there to do. Remember that change in the outer world around you can only be sustained if your inner world is the stronger of the two.

Another question I am often asked is what is the difference between imagination and intuition. In using your intuition you stop seeing with your mind what you think should be there. Instead you tune in with your heart to feel what is really there. Your intuition is the voice of your higher self but you must calm your emotions and quieten your mind to hear it. You know when it is your imagination because it comes with thoughts, opinions and judgements. In other words you are coming from your mind which 'houses' all your fears and past experiences. Whenever you question your interpretation of a situation then you are coming from your imagination; you are constantly reshaping and justifying your thoughts about the situation. Your intuition, on the other hand, is the quiet sense of feeling and knowing something to be true.

Come and have fun
As my dad would say, "Let's go have some fun!" Take time to laugh. Play with these universal laws and learn the secrets of our Universe. Love yourself and become your own best friend by exploring who you really are. Choose to take responsibility for your life. Become aware of what you do to yourself and change direction if necessary. Ask and then listen for the signs from the Universe. But most importantly,

connect with your soul and live within that space. Then you will experience the spirit world and all your wishes and your dreams will manifest in your outer world.

Please go and play with the fairies at the bottom of your garden. Have fun with your life – it is there patiently waiting for you.

Spook Terminology

Some of the following terms which I have used throughout this book to describe particular situations or experiences may have other meanings. These are just my personal interpretations.

Channel:
the line of communication used to connect with the soul, the spiritual realms and spiritual world.

Clairaudience:
a means by which one is able to hear messages from the spiritual realms and spiritual world.

Clairsentience:
the ability to feel a person's energy field.

Clairvoyance:
the means by which one is able to see images of situations and circumstances surrounding a person's energy field.

Energy field:
the sum total of thoughts and emotions which radiate out into the physical world; the vibration of the energy field can be

altered by changing thoughts and emotions.

Energy transference:
the transference of energy between one person and another which initiates a realisation for one or both of them.

Inner world:
the inner reality or essence of a person, related to the heart not the head; a place where one can meditate and observe the self.

Outer world:
the physical world that exists outside the individual; a world in which you can't change anything; a world that exists only in the past.

Personality:
the mind or part of a person's psyche that operates in the physical world and feels pain and negative emotions like jealousy and anger.

Physical world:
the world of the body, mind and emotions where the personality feels, thinks and takes action; a world that is often full of emotions, judgements and opinions.

Soul:
the spiritual or immortal part of an individual, which has all the memories, accomplishments and achievements since time began. Each soul knows the lessons available for the next step forward. The soul is energy and is connected to universal energy.

Soul space:
when I am in my soul space, I am in love. This is where I connect with the spiritual world and spiritual realms. To achieve this, I blank my mind and remove all aspects of my personality.

Spiritual world:
the world where the soul or higher self resides. It is a world full of love and soul qualities.

Universe:
the Universe is what we are all part of; it is a state of moving energy, which responds to our individual thoughts, emotions and actions.

Universal laws:
these laws form the foundation of the spiritual and physical worlds. They are immutable and whether the individual is aware of them or not, they govern everything in life. They provide the order within the Universe that keeps everything flowing perfectly. They are the guideline for life itself.

Universal love:
I always feel that the Universe is held together with love and therefore, it is within everything. I know this love is always present even within my biggest challenges.